BIRDS OF PREY

Look for these and other books in the
Lucent Endangered Animals and Habitats Series:

The Amazon Rain Forest
The Bald Eagle
Birds of Prey
The Bear
Coral Reefs
The Elephant
The Giant Panda
The Gorilla
The Manatee
The Oceans
The Orangutan
The Rhinoceros
Seals and Sea Lions
The Shark
The Tiger
The Whale
The Wolf

Other related titles in the Lucent Overview Series:

Acid Rain
Endangered Species
Energy Alternatives
Garbage
The Greenhouse Effect
Hazardous Waste
Ocean Pollution
Oil Spills
Ozone
Pesticides
Population
Rainforests
Recycling
Saving the American Wilderness
Vanishing Wetlands
Zoos

BIRDS OF PREY

BY KELLY L. BARTH

Endangered
Animals &
Habitats

LUCENT BOOKS, INC.
SAN DIEGO, CALIFORNIA

Library of Congress Cataloging-in-Publication Data

Barth, Kelly L.
    Birds of prey / by Kelly L. Barth
       p.   cm. — (Endangered animals & habitats)
    Includes bibliographical references and index.
    Summary: Discusses birds of prey and their endangered status,
including the problem of pesticides, the struggle for space and
resources, breeding in captivity and reintroduction to the wild, and
worldwide recovery efforts.
    ISBN 1-56006-493-5 (lib. bdg. : alk. paper)
    1. Birds of Prey—Juvenile literature. 2. Endangered species—
Juvenile literature.   [1. Birds of Prey. 2. Endangered species.]
I. Title. II. Series.
  QL696.F3B38   2000
  598.9—dc21   99-38326
                                             CIP

Copyright © 2000 by Lucent Books, Inc.
P.O. Box 289011, San Diego, CA 92198-9011
Printed in the U.S.A.

Contents

Introduction

BIRDS OF PREY, or raptors as they are also known, have universally proved a source of fascination. For thousands of years, humans have admired the beauty of a bird of prey as it soars high over the ground, swooping, or diving toward its prey. These swift, powerful, independent creatures are so named because they are predators; they hunt, kill, and eat other animals.

Because of their strength, self-sufficiency, and mystery, birds of prey have played a significant role in the mythology of many cultures. For example, pictures of the birds appear on currency and national seals of nations throughout the world. Birds such as the Andean condor, the Philippine eagle, and the bald eagle have been named national symbols. Sports teams sometimes adopt birds of prey as their mascot because of the bird's reputed strength or courage.

Humans have come to see birds of prey in a practical way as well, since they serve a crucial role in maintaining nature's balance. If birds of prey did not eat small mammals, for example, the populations of these little animals would grow to the point where they would deplete their own food supply. This natural control of animal populations often directly benefits humans as well. Birds of prey feed on birds, rodents, insects, and small mammals that eat and damage food crops. Raptors keep the populations of these animals in check naturally, reducing the need for pesticides and poisons.

The bald eagle, long admired for its beauty and grace, glides majestically through the air.

Threats to birds of prey

Despite their usefulness to humankind, in the last century raptor populations around the world have experienced significant decreases. Scientists concerned about the drop in numbers have investigated the problem to determine reasons for it. They have discovered that the primary reason for the decline in raptor populations is the loss of habitat and resources to growing human populations. Birds of prey need large territories with healthy and abundant supplies of prey. Humans have increasingly occupied land needed by raptors and the animals they prey upon, especially in the last few decades. Once their habitat has been lost to development by humans, individual birds often have difficulty finding another area not already occupied by another of its species.

Another serious threat to birds of prey is the continuing effect of pesticides. Pesticides can affect birds of prey in a number of ways, but the most harmful is that such chemicals interfere with their ability to reproduce. Though some pesticides have been banned by various governments because of their effect on birds of prey, many harmful chemicals are still in use.

Birds of prey such as the burrowing owl compete with humans for habitat.

Many populations of raptors have also declined as a direct result of human attack. People and birds of prey sometimes rely on the same resources for food and habitat. Moreover, some people who make their living directly from the land or who hunt the same prey as raptors see the birds as competitors that must be removed.

Currently, many species of birds of prey are in danger of becoming extinct. The continued loss of habitat and resources coupled with already reduced populations means that many species may not survive, despite any effort to save them. In some cases, helping a raptor population recover in an area where it is bound to lose even more habitat and resources doesn't make sense. If allowed to proceed at its current pace, development of open land by humans will make it nearly impossible for some raptor species to survive.

Hope for the future

The picture is not entirely bleak though. As humans have become more aware of the plight of birds of prey, they have taken steps to correct problems they created. In response, populations of some endangered raptors have increased. Conservationists have learned how to raise some endangered birds of prey in captivity and reintroduce them to their former habitat. Corporations and individuals have set aside land to preserve habitat and agreed to conduct their businesses and lives in ways that leave room for threatened species. Public education efforts are showing people all over the world the importance of raptor species to ecological balance. Nations are beginning to cooperate with one another to protect raptor species that migrate across national boundaries.

Conservationists hope these combined efforts will help the world continue to be a place where some birds of prey can live wild and free. Whether this will be possible remains to be seen.

1

What Is a Bird of Prey?

BIRDS OF PREY have lived on the earth for a long time. The fossil remains of their oldest known ancestor date back 70 million years. Called the *Diatryma steini,* the creature was six to seven feet tall and a ground dweller. Ancient birds of prey thrived, and today, descendants of this ancient species now live on every continent except Antarctica.

Orders and families

Birds of prey are grouped into categories by a scientific system of classification called taxonomy. On the most basic level, birds of prey are divided into two divisions or orders, the Falconiformes and the Strigiformes. The Falconiformes are diurnal or daytime fliers and hunters. Hawks, eagles, falcons, and vultures all belong to this order. Strigiformes are nocturnal or nighttime birds of prey. Owls are the only living members of this order.

Each order is further broken down into groupings called families. The family Accipitridae is made up of buteos, accipiters, harriers, kites, eagles, and Old World vultures. The family Falconidae includes falcons, merlins, and kestrels. The family Carthartidae includes the New World vultures. The order Strigiforme is broken up into two families, the Tytonidae and the Strigidae. The family Tytonidae contains barn and bay owls, and the family Strigidae contains all other owls.

Characteristics in common

The fundamental trait all birds of prey share is that they feed primarily on meat. Whether they hunt and kill their food or feed on the carcasses of dead animals, all birds of prey have excellent vision and hearing and the strength necessary to find and eat their food. (Interestingly, no bird of prey needs to drink. They get all the water they need from the bodies of their prey.)

Birds of prey do not chew their food. Instead, they swallow pieces torn from the body or simply swallow the prey whole. To rid their bodies of undigestible matter, raptors' digestive systems form small oblong masses called pellets or casts containing the hair, bone, and nails of their prey.

Exaggerated Fears

People have long feared the size and hunting prowess of raptors. Though no recorded accounts of raptors attacking human beings exist, myths grew up that fed upon peoples' fear of these powerful, wild creatures so clearly outside the realm of domestication and control. As Bruce Beans describes in the following passage from his book *Eagle's Plume,* even books written for school children perpetuated such fears:

Only a bird whose image has been so pumped up by centuries of public relations jabberwocky could be considered capable of the legendary feats that have been attributed to eagles. . . . One of the most pervasive, influential examples of this mythmaking was disseminated by McGuffey's Readers, the grade school series whose dramatic, highly moralistic tales heavily influenced the teaching of reading in this country between 1840 and 1920. Among the stories read by millions of American children was "The Eagle's Nest," which involved an evil golden eagle spiriting away a young child to its eyrie atop a steep mountain in Scotland. With a crowd of a thousand amassed below, the girl's mother does what no man would dare—she scales the cliff. As in many of these tales (and a good indication that they are indeed fiction), when she reaches her daughter the child is completely unharmed and unmarked by piercing talon wounds.

Another feature raptors have in common is that one sex is larger and stronger than the other, a phenomenon called "sexual dimorphism." In the case of raptors, usually the females are bigger. Scientists have suggested a reason for the size difference. Raptor specialist Philip Callahan describes the theory: "The male bringing food to the nest is presumably reluctant to release the food to the female and young. Since the female dominates, she is better able to intimidate the male to release the prey if she is larger."[1]

All raptors perform elaborate mating rituals. In preparation for breeding, these birds may spiral into the air, dive, and chase each other. On the ground they may bow to each other, touch beaks, and feed and preen one another. Researchers and amateur naturalists alike have observed birds of prey such as the bald eagle carry out spectacular courtship aerobatics. While one flies upside down, extending a talon, the other grasps that talon with its own, and the two cartwheel to earth, releasing just before they hit the ground. Displays such as this doubtless help enshrine raptors in humans' imaginations, motivating people to help protect these majestic creatures.

Northern goshawks, like all birds of prey, rely on their extraordinary vision, hearing, and strength to successfully hunt for food.

Endangered species legislation

As environmental changes on the earth have made it increasingly difficult for birds of prey to survive, efforts are being made to protect species whose populations have dropped to low levels. Some of the most important protective measures have come in the form of legislation. For example, the U.S. Endangered Species Act, a law passed in 1973, gives protection to animals in danger of becoming extinct. International agreements reached in the 1970s protect such species in similar ways.

Within the Endangered Species Act, endangered animals are distinguished from threatened ones. To be listed as endangered, a species must be in danger of extinction through most of its natural range. An animal is listed as threatened because it stands a good chance of becoming endangered in the near future. Many of the birds of prey have been classified as endangered according to definitions determined by governments or international environmental groups. The dangers faced by birds of prey are many; few, if any, of the families of birds of prey are free from danger.

Hawks

The term "hawk" is the common name generally given to a group of efficient hunting birds. Hawks are members of the order Falconiforme and the family Accipitridae. Within the common classification of hawk, two of the groups containing the largest numbers of species are buteos and accipiters.

Buteos have long, broad wings which allow them to move over large territories of open country by soaring, which takes much less effort than flapping. Some examples of buteos are the red-tailed, broad-winged, red-shouldered, and Swainson's hawks.

The broad wings of the red-tailed hawk enable it to soar high over open countryside.

Accipiters, on the other hand, have adapted to living in forest habitats. Sometimes called bird hawks because of their ability to catch other birds in flight, accipters have short, rounded wings that allow them to fly rapidly through trees and close in on their prey. An accipiter's long tail aids it in maneuvering through the close quarters of its forest habitat. Northern goshawks, Cooper's hawks, and sharp-shinned hawks are good examples of accipiters.

Another smaller group of hawks are the kites. Kites are recognizable by their long, narrow wings and tails and by their distinct way of flying that makes them appear to float in the air. These insect-eating hawks live in or near marshes and wetland areas. The Mississippi kite is a well-known North American example from this group.

The Cooper's hawk belongs to a family of birds that makes its home primarily in forested regions.

Hawks can be distinguished from other birds of prey by their size and shape. They range from one and a half to two feet in height, and, on average, they weigh about two pounds. Hawks have heavily feathered legs and long, narrow toes. They also have short, hooked beaks.

Another characteristic shared by hawks is eyesight uniquely adapted to their needs. They have binocular vision, which means they can see the same object with both eyes, allowing them to judge the distance of objects accurately. Hawks have a wide range of monocular vision as well, which means that each eye can see objects to the side that the other cannot see. Because of this combination of monocular and binocular vision, hawks can see nearly all around themselves without turning their heads. Such acute and wide vision allows hawks to be skillful hunters.

Hunting techniques vary among hawks. Buteos, for example, drop quickly on their prey after having spotted it from high in the air. They eat anything they can overpower, including rodents, small mammals, reptiles, and insects. The fast-flying accipiter, on the other hand, often catches its bird prey in flight and returns to a roost to kill and eat it.

Once they have captured their prey, all hawks, regardless of their species, kill it in much the same way. Both buteos and accipiters kill their prey with their sharp, hooked beaks. Depending on the size of the kill, a hawk may swallow its prey whole, or it may tear pieces of flesh from the body and swallow them.

Though their nests differ between species, all hawks choose sites that are out of reach of predators and provide a good vantage point to search for prey. Many hawks build nests high in a tree or reuse those that have been built by other raptors. Other hawks build their nests on a cliff or rocky ledge. Most hawk nests consist of large sticks arranged with a slight bowl shape in the center that they line with soft materials such as leaves, roots, grasses, down from their own breast, lichen, or even human-made materials, such as bits of string. Many species return to the same nest year after year, repairing it where necessary.

Hawks must provide enough food for themselves and their young, so they put up fierce fights during nesting season to protect their nesting territory from other individuals of their species. Between nesting seasons, however, most hawks can quite happily share the same territory with others of their species. It is not uncommon to see two hawks sharing the same roosting tree, in fact.

Depending on the species, hawks generally lay from two to five spotted, oval-shaped eggs in the nest. The female incubates them for about one month. The chicks generally remain in the nest about six to seven weeks. Their parents bring them prey and tear pieces of flesh from the bodies for them to swallow. At about four to five weeks, the young grow substantial wing feathers. Like many other birds of prey, a hawk youngster spends the last few weeks in the nest learning to tear food with its talons and beak and flapping its wings to strengthen them for flight.

Eagles

"Eagle" is the common name given to members of the group containing the largest and most powerful birds of prey. Like their cousins the hawks, they belong to the order

Moral Judgment of the Eagle

Throughout history, many people have judged animals by moral codes constructed by humans. Such judgments sometimes reveal a lack of understanding of the challenges animals face in surviving an often harsh natural world. Birds of prey are no exception. For example, in his book, *Eagle's Plume,* Bruce Beans notes that Benjamin Franklin had the following to say about the bald eagle during discussions about whether it should be designated as the national bird of the United States:

> I wish the Bald Eagle had not been chosen as the Representative of our Country. He is a Bird of bad moral Character. He does not get his Living honestly. You may have seen him perch'd on some dead Tree near the River, where, too lazy to fish for himself, he watches the Labour of the Fishing Hawk; and, when that diligent Bird has at length taken a Fish, and is bearing it to his Nest for the Support of his Mate and young Ones, the Bald Eagle pursues him and takes it from him. With all this Injustice, he is never in good Case but like those among Men who live by Sharping and Robbing he is generally poor and often very lousy.

During discussions about choosing a national bird, Ben Franklin had little praise for the bald eagle.

Falconiforme and the family Accipitridae. Some of the best-known eagles include the bald and golden eagles of North America, the harpy eagle of South America, the Philippine eagle, and the Spanish imperial eagle.

Though each species of eagle varies somewhat in appearance, an observer can look for a couple of characteristics to determine that a raptor is an eagle. The most obvious of these characteristics is its large size. On average, eagles are about three feet long. Those that live in open country, such as the golden eagle, can have wingspans of up to seven feet. Forest eagles like the harpy generally have shorter rounded wings that make it easier for them to fly through the trees, but they still are quite large.

Along with large bodies, eagles have the biggest and strongest feet of all of the birds of prey. With toes outstretched, an eagle's feet can be as large as a human hand. Eagles need these powerful feet to kill and carry heavy prey to their roost or nest.

The harpy eagle, like other eagles, is a swift and powerful hunter.

Eagles are powerful hunters. They swoop down on their prey and pierce and kill it with their talons. With their beaks, eagles tear, cut, and grind the bones and flesh of their prey. Depending on the region where an eagle lives, it may eat rodents, large birds, fish, the carcasses of dead animals, or even large mammals such as sheep, antelope, or monkeys.

These large birds need sturdy expansive nests to accommodate a nesting pair and two to three nestlings. Called eyries, eagles' nests are usually built in remote, high trees or on cliffs far from where humans live. Though eagles most often use large sticks for the bases of their nests, they have been known to use broomsticks, lumber, and animal bones as well. The nests are lined with moss, leaves, and other soft materials. An eyrie can measure as much as ten feet across and twenty feet deep, because eagles often return to the same nest site year after year, adding fresh nest materials to it. One well-used eyrie found by researchers measured twenty feet deep and weighed an astounding three tons!

Most eagles mate for life, which helps them become experienced, protective parents. Once the eagle pair settles in a nest, the female usually lays one or two speckled eggs that will hatch in about a month. The parents take turns feeding their young. After the eaglets are about six weeks old, the parents stop bringing them as much food to encourage them to leave the nest. The hungry eaglets begin to take practice flights so they can follow their parents to the prey they have caught. Both the male and female feed and teach the young until they are experienced enough to hunt on their own.

An adult eagle (above) is a proficient hunter. It encourages its young (left) to fly from their nest at an early age in preparation for hunting.

Its aerodynamic body and tail allow the peregrine falcon to dive faster than any other bird of prey.

Falcons

Though falcons belong to the same order (Falconiforme) as hawks, these smaller raptors actually belong to a different family, the Falconidae. Examples of falcons are merlins, peregrines, and kestrels.

Falcons share several characteristics that distinguish them from hawks. These small birds of prey have long, thin wings, large heads, big-shouldered bodies and square tails that give them a distinct look. They can also be identified from a distance by their unique flight. Unlike other birds of prey, falcons often hover in the air in preparation for a sudden and precise dive onto their prey.

More than other birds of prey, falcons are uniquely equipped to dive at great speeds. During a dive or "stoop," as it is known, a falcon folds its wings tight against its body, reducing wind resistance. Naturalist Peter Parnall describes this little raptor's flying speed: "When diving, the falcon exceeds any bird in speed. Some experts say it can fly in excess of two hundred miles an hour."[2] This speedy little bird is an excellent hunter. Unlike other birds of prey, a falcon does not kill its prey with its feet and talons. Instead, it knocks its prey from the air or off its feet and kills with its beak. The short, hooked beak has a structure on each side that a falcon uses to break the spine of its prey. Depending on the species and the region where it lives, a falcon might eat small birds, rodents, snakes, or insects.

As a rule, most falcons prefer nesting on ledges, either natural or manmade. For example, the peregrine falcon thrives in urban environments, nesting high up on buildings. Falcons are not known for putting a great deal of effort into building a nest. Most simply scratch together a pile of available debris such as leaves and rocks and then lay their eggs on it.

A falcon generally lays three to five small, speckled eggs in the nest, where the female will then incubate them. Though small and helpless at first, the young grow feathers

The Rise and Fall of Falconry

Humans sought early on to harness the keen hunting skills of birds of prey. Falcons, hawks, and even eagles have been hand-reared and trained to kill small birds and mammals for their trainers, called falconers. Historical records indicate that as early as 3000 years ago, people in China and Persia tamed birds of prey and trained them to kill and bring back food for them to eat. This practice may have been the beginnings of falconry, a sport still practiced on a small scale today. Early mentions of falconry in Greece date back to 400 B.C.

Throughout Europe during the Middle Ages, falconry flourished, and elaborate laws were written to govern it. Many books were printed detailing the privileges of certain individual participants. For example, a person's rank, such as king, prince, duke, or earl, determined the size and type of hunting bird he could own. Theft of a hunting bird was taken very seriously, since by stealing a hawk, a thief could literally keep a man from supplying food for himself and his family. By the decree of King Edward III of England, stealing a hawk became a crime punishable by death.

As humans began to rely on guns for hunting game, interest in falconry naturally declined. Even today, however, some still appreciate the months of hard work put into training a bird to hunt for its trainer.

within about three weeks and can pull bits of meat from the prey that their parents bring them. Some falcons, like the peregrine, coax their young to fly and teach them to hunt by releasing the prey into the air for them to catch.

Vultures

All of the world's vultures, a common name for the group that includes condors as well, belong to the order Falconi-forme. These large birds of prey, however, are divided into two families according to the geographic region they inhabit. Old World vultures, which live in Europe, Asia, and Africa, belong to the family Accipitridae. Examples of Old

An Andean condor perches among the trees. Condors and vultures feed almost entirely on dead and decaying animals.

World vultures include the European cinereous vulture, Spain's griffon vulture, and the hooded and cape vultures of Africa. New World vultures, which live in North and South America, belong to the family Cathartidae. The well-known California condor belongs to this family, as does the Andean condor and black and turkey vultures. The two families of vultures are very much alike except that the slightly larger New World vultures do not build nests as Old World vultures do.

The well-known circling flight of a vulture is different from that of other birds of prey. Instead of relying on flapping alone, these raptors use their broad wings to take advantage of updrafts of warm air called thermals. They can circle high in the air for hours, searching for food. This mode of flying works quite well, allowing the birds to soar as high as four miles and achieve speeds exceeding one hundred miles per hour.

The primary difference, however, between vultures and other birds of prey is that vultures feed almost entirely on carrion, the dead bodies of other animals, rather than on prey they have killed themselves. In fact, most vultures could not kill live prey even if they wanted to because they lack the strength in their feet or sharpness in their talons that would be needed in making a kill.

Vultures are uniquely adapted to feeding on carcasses. When they eat, they brace their feet against a carcass and thrust their heads into it, tearing bits of flesh from it with their hooked beaks. Because vultures have no feathers on their heads and necks, they can easily rub blood and decaying food onto the ground and then bathe their skin in streams and rivers. They can eat decaying meat because enzymes in their digestive systems kill disease-causing bacteria.

Though New World vultures do not build nests, mating pairs do search for just the right spot to lay their eggs and take an interest in parenting. They lay their eggs on cliffs and in caves and hollow trees. Some vultures may even lay their eggs on the ground, which though it may seem a careless place to put them, is usually in a spot protected from predators that might eat them. Ground-nesting vultures such as the black vulture have been known to throw shiny objects such as tin foil scraps or broken glass around the nest. Old World Vultures, on the other hand, build stick nests, often lining them with the fur from their prey. Their nests are large and rest in branches at the tops of tall trees, far out of reach of predators.

Both male and female vultures participate actively in nesting and in raising young. Female vultures incubate their eggs for about one month, feeding on regurgitated food brought to them by the male. After the chicks hatch, their parents regurgitate food which the chicks eat by pushing their beaks inside their parents' beaks.

Young vultures remain with their parents longer than the young of other raptors. In most species, not until the chicks have been in the nest about five months are they ready to leave the nest and hunt with their parents. Though most are completely self-sufficient by six months of age, some, like the condors of North and South America, are guarded and fed by their parents until they reach two years of age. This may be one reason such species breed only every two years, instead of every year like other birds of prey.

Vultures feed on a carcass in Kenya, Africa.

The barn owl, distinguishable by its heart-shaped face, is most active at night.

Owls

Owls belong to a different order than all the other birds of prey, the order Strigiforme. Within this order are two families. The barn and bay owls, which have heart-shaped faces and are smaller and darker than other owls, belong to the family Tytonidae. All other owls belong to the family Strigidae and can be distinguished from the barn and bay owls by their rounded faces and large eyes. Examples of this type of owl include the great horned, screech, and barred owls.

Owls have excellent eyesight. Unlike the other birds of prey that hunt during the day, owls are "nocturnal," meaning they are most active at night. Although owls have excellent night vision, they also see perfectly well in the daylight. Owls have binocular vision like humans with eyes that both face forward on their relatively flat faces. This allows them to see the same object with both eyes and accurately judge the distance of their prey. Numerous neck muscles allow owls to turn their heads 270 degrees. By turning the head, they can see things beside and even behind them. As naturalist Angus Cameron says, "So fast is this motion, that many an observer has sworn the owl can turn his head completely around."[3]

Owls rely on their hearing as well as vision. Thanks to their excellent hearing, owls can hunt in almost complete darkness. One ear is located higher on the head than the other, an arrangement scientists call aural asymmetry. This adaptation functions a little like radar, and helps owls judge distance as they fly toward their prey. Owls also have a facial disk of feathers that funnels sound toward their ears, helping them hear even the slightest movement of their prey.

An owl's feathers also contribute to their hunting success in other ways. Most owls have feathers that camou-

Eagle, Vultures, and Owls in Myth and Symbol

Because of their strength and beauty, eagles have filled the imaginations and myths of humans. They are prominent symbols for many religious traditions. For example, the Lakota Sioux consider an eagle's presence at their Sun Dance ceremony a blessing and believe that the eagle will carry their prayers to heaven. The eagle was also associated by ancient Greeks with Zeus, the god of the sky, and by Romans with the god Jupiter.

Like eagles, vultures figure prominently in the myths of many cultures. The ancient Incas saw them as messengers to the gods. Native Americans of the west coast of the United States believed that the California condor caused the thunder, because of the deep resonant sounds their wings make in flight. Even today, some people of the Chumash tribe believe that if the California condor becomes extinct their tribe will die out as well.

Mysterious night flyers, owls have also inspired a strange mixture of fear and respect in humans throughout the centuries. Assumed by many cultures to be especially wise, the owl was associated with Athena, the Greek goddess of wisdom. The Aztecs, on the other hand, associated the owl with their god of the dead.

Though seen by some as a sign of danger or doom, owls have also been portrayed as strong helpers in warding off evil. For example, the Altaic people in Central Asia in early times would hang pictures of owls in a child's bedroom in order to repel evil spirits. Similarly, people in Japan collected sculptures of owls to fight off sickness and famine.

flage them so that potential prey cannot easily spot them. Also, an owl's feathers have soft, toothed edges which silence the sound of air flowing over their wings. Thanks to this adaptation, an owl's prey usually does not even hear it swoop down to catch it.

Unlike the other birds of prey, which spend a great deal of hunting time in flight, owls spot their prey from a roost and then swoop down on it. They use little energy soaring above the ground searching for prey. Instead, they use a burst of energy for a swift, accurate dive onto prey that they have used their keen eyes and ears to spot from their perch.

Young owls are sometimes pushed from their nests by older siblings. This naturally controls the number of owls in the wilderness.

Owls' diets are quite varied. Depending on its size and location, an owl might eat rodents, larger mammals like rabbits and skunks, large birds, or insects. For example, small species like the screech owl eat mainly small rodents or insects, while larger species like the barn owl would eat larger prey such as rabbits.

Surprisingly, an owl can open its small-looking mouth wide enough to swallow all but its largest prey whole. Since owls, like all of the birds of prey, do not need to chew their food, this method of eating is quite efficient.

Owls raise their young in a variety of places, depending on the species, but rarely in nests they construct themselves. They might lay their eggs in a hollow tree, in the abandoned nest of another kind of bird, or even in a depression in the ground. The choice of nesting sites is often determined by the food supply. For example, barn and screech owls lay their eggs on level surfaces in airy structures such as barns or old steeples, most likely because of a plentiful supply of rodents that such structures attract.

Owls lay each of their three to six eggs a few days apart, which naturally controls the number of owls that survive each season. The owlets that hatch first become larger and eat more food than their smaller nest mates. The larger owlets might even push smaller ones from the nest. Sometimes only two survive from a nesting period. This automatic population control is necessary because of the difficulty young owls have in locating an open territory and finding enough food to eat.

Struggling to live together

Regardless of the species, birds of prey are threatened by competition with humans. As human populations grow in many countries, the need for food, shelter, and transportation increases as well. Whether intentional or not, human disturbance of the habitats for birds of prey can interfere with them so much that they have difficulty hunting, nesting, and reproducing. Of the many things threatening the survival of birds of prey, loss of habitat and food resources to humans presents the biggest problem. Many raptor species have declined as a direct result of the struggle with humans over the world's limited open space. In addition, some of the by-products of human activity directly affect birds of prey.

2

The Problem
of Pesticides

THROUGHOUT MOST OF the twentieth century, humans have used chemicals called pesticides to protect themselves and their crops from damage and disease caused by other living things. Pesticides are applied to agricultural crops and human environments to eliminate a number of problems: insects, fungi, weeds, or rodents. Depending on what they are used for, pesticides may be called insecticides, fungicides, herbicides, or rodenticides.

Pesticides have provided many benefits to humans. By controlling insects, they have played a major role in controlling insect-borne diseases such as malaria, typhus, and the plague. No longer do people have to worry about becoming ill from eating grain contaminated by fungi. Also, pesticides have allowed humans to meet the needs of their increasing populations by allowing them to produce more food per acre of land than was possible in the past.

Along with these benefits though, pesticide use also has had serious drawbacks. For example, some pesticides still used today have been found to be poisonous to both people and animals who eat, inhale, or touch them. In some cases, if not treated after exposure to pesticides, they can die.

Another disadvantage of pesticides is their persistence. Once present in the tissues of animals, the soil or the water supply, pesticides can remain there for a long time. They often initially enter rivers, lakes, and groundwater as rainwater washes them from agricultural fields. Residual

Pesticide spraying can be costly to both humans and animals. Pesticides can contaminate water and harm living organisms all the way up the food chain.

amounts of these chemicals can linger in soil and water for years, and clean-up can be a costly, time-consuming process. Similarly, some pesticides remain in the body tissues of humans and animals for many years after their initial exposure to them. Even worse, pesticides can be passed up the food chain as larger creatures prey on smaller ones contaminated by the chemicals.

The most visible victims of pesticides

Most often, pesticides enter a raptor's body when it consumes contaminated prey. In fact, because birds of prey live high on the food chain, eating many insects, birds, fish, reptiles, or mammals already contaminated by pesticides, they are some of the first visible victims of these chemicals. For example, vultures can be contaminated by feeding on the carcass of a coyote that died feeding on a rodent killed by pesticides. Similarly, the same pesticide that contaminates the fish swimming in pesticide-laden waters in turn finds its way into the body tissues of eagles that eat the fish.

As a group, raptors eat such a variety of other creatures that they provide a good indication of the extent to which the chemicals have contaminated the environment. As John Love describes in his book *Return of the Sea Eagle* about the effects of pesticides on sea eagle populations in Great Britain, predatory birds act as an "indicator species." That is, they are animals whose health problems warn humans of the subtle effects they too may already be experiencing because an environmental problem has not been addressed: "Being at the top of the food chain in that environment, and extremely sensitive to such chemicals, predatory birds provided an early warning that immediate and appropriate steps were necessary to avert global disaster."[4]

In some instances, raptors are especially at risk because they may be attracted by the struggles of prey animals poisoned by pesticides. For example, one chemical poured onto perches near fish farms in Florida to kill nuisance birds and insects contaminates small birds that absorb the pesticides through their feet. When the small birds leave the perches, the problem begins for raptors. As naturalist Ted Williams notes, "Poisoned birds fly off in up to 10-

---

 Raptor Deaths Ignored

Even in the United States, with its reputation as a worldwide leader in environmental awareness, little attention has been paid to deaths of birds of prey as a result of pesticides. Though the government ban on DDT has benefited many raptors, including the bald eagle, such benefits were not planned. The primary reason for the banning of DDT was an effort to respond to discoveries about its effect on humans. For decades before, birds of prey declined as a result of the use of the chemical. Rather than seeing raptor deaths and reproductive problems as a warning for humans, governments have historically seen such deaths as an inevitable price to pay for agricultural progress. In his article "Silent Scourge," nature writer Ted Williams had this to say:

> despite the well-documented lethal and sublethal effects of pesticides on bird life, never has the EPA banned a pesticide for any reason other than presumed danger to people. Even DDT was banned for sale in the United States not because it nearly caused the extinction of bald eagles, ospreys, peregrine falcons . . . but because in 1971 the National Institutes of Health found DDT or its breakdown products in 100 percent of the human-tissue samples it examined.

Despite complaints about pesticide-related animal deaths, certain pesticides were not banned until their toxic effect was studied on humans.

mile radii, then bounce around on the ground in their death throes, attracting raptors. . . . If a poison is capable of killing birds merely by contacting the tough epidermal lining of their feet, you can imagine what it can do to a raptor when absorbed by digestive system tissues."[5]

Birds of prey populations can also decline because their members come into direct contact with pesticides. For instance, a raptor can quickly die after preening its feathers and ingesting chemicals that collect on its body during spray application of pesticides. Some raptors are known for following behind as farmers plow their fields and stir up insects in the process. Unfortunately, the farmers often are also spraying pesticides at the same time, and that spray contaminates the birds' feathers.

Pesticides' effect on raptors

Pesticides do not always kill an exposed raptor quickly, but instead weaken its central nervous system. As a result, these usually skilled and intelligent birds develop poor vision and motor skills, making them less able to fly around obstacles such as vehicles and power lines. In fact, the initial cause of many injuries to birds of prey that arrive at wildlife rehabilitation centers can be traced to pesticides

A black-necked stilt shows some of the harmful effects of chemical contamination.

that weakened their central nervous systems. Ed Clark, president of the Wildlife Center of Virginia speaks from first-hand experience: "How . . . does an eagle that can see its prey from a mile away manage to get hit by a tractor trailer truck? The overwhelming majority of birds we treat have been poisoned first."[6] Also, pesticides can so damage the nervous system of southern or northern migrating raptors that they mistakenly travel to places where they cannot survive or reproduce because of inappropriate climate or insufficient habitat or food.

Pesticides can also cause central nervous system problems that directly lead to a raptor's death. Naturalist Ted Williams says that common pesticides such as organophosphates and carbamates "short-circuit an organism's nervous system by binding with an enzyme that controls electrical impulses . . . throughout the body. Muscles contract in random sequence, and the victim usually dies of respiratory failure."[7] Often, however, the effects of pesticides are much less immediate and so subtle that they go unnoticed for decades.

Pesticides cause raptors long-term damage by interfering with their ability to reproduce and rear their young. A pesticide can affect a raptor's reproductive system in several ways. The chemicals can thin the eggshells so that the nesting parent crushes the developing embryo. Also, pesticides can create deformities in the developing embryo so that even if the young raptor does hatch, it cannot survive to adulthood. Finally, young birds can starve to death in the nest, a result of their parents being too weakened to care for them adequately. The effect of a class of pesticides known as chlorinated hydrocarbons is a case in point.

DDT: Chlorinated hydrocarbons and their victims

Though use of chlorinated hydrocarbons did lead to bigger and healthier crop harvests and a decline in the diseases spread by insects, the efficiency of these pesticides was gradually overshadowed by hints of their toxic effects on the environment and on many creatures they were not intended to affect. Chlorinated hydrocarbons (chlorine combined with the organic compound hydrocarbon) are human-made chemicals that kill insects and other creatures that eat them by interfering with normal nerve function. The most commonly used chlorinated hydrocarbon was dichloro-diphenyl-trichloroethane (DDT). The dangers this compound posed to birds and other animals were known early on. In 1945, conservationist Richard Pough, who participated in government experiments testing the effects of DDT on forest birds, said, "If DDT should ever be used widely and without care, we would have a country without fresh water, fish, serpents, frogs, and most of the birds we have now."[8]

Not only are they deadly, but chlorinated hydrocarbon pesticides are very stable, meaning they do not break down into less harmful chemicals but instead remain intact for years in the soil and water where they have been applied. Not surprisingly, scientists also discovered that they remained intact in the fatty tissues of creatures that came in contact with them as well. Specifically, scientists discovered chlorinated hydrocarbons in the fatty tissues of the bodies of America's national bird, the bald eagle, whose diet consisted primarily of fish that had eaten other animals living in rivers contaminated with DDT.

DDT: A Blessing and a Curse

Invented in 1874, DDT (dichloro-diphenyl-trichloroethane) came into wide use during World War II when it was applied to soldiers' uniforms to kill insects such as lice that could spread disease. Inexpensive and simple to manufacture, DDT effectively controlled the spread of many insect-borne diseases in countries around the world. In the late 1940s and early 1950s, scientists realized that DDT and other so-called "hard" insecticides do not break down into less toxic forms but remain intact in the environment, where they can contaminate living things sometimes years after their initial application.

DDT endangers the bald eagle

Research revealed that the problem with chlorinated hydrocarbons was widespread, but subtle in the way birds were affected. Throughout the 1950s and 1960s, U.S. scientists discovered that DDT had "thoroughly infiltrated the food chain, severely affecting the reproduction of many predatory birds,"[9] including the bald eagle. Chlorinated hydrocarbons interfered primarily with the bald eagle's calcium metabolism. Bird eggshells are made principally of calcium, so the shells of the eggs laid by pesticide-affected eagles were too thin to hold up under the weight of a nesting parent. The number of bald eagle eggshells crushed before eaglets could hatch played a significant role in the bird's population decline. Fortunately, legislators and government regulators took action before the eagles were wiped out.

Bald eagle recovery

Two factors helped slow the bald eagle's decline: passage of laws regulating the use of chlorinated hydrocarbons and nationwide recovery efforts. Passage of the U.S. National Environmental Policy Act in 1969 and a campaign initiated by the Environmental Defense Fund and the National Audubon Society led to the banning of all domestic uses of DDT in 1972. When the U.S. Endangered Species Act was passed the following year, the bald eagle was one of the first added to the list. Conservation groups provided supplemental feeding stations for eagles and constructed temporary housing for them as well. Gradually, these efforts to help the bird recover paid off.

Arguably, bald eagles have made a significant recovery, given the real threat they faced in the middle part of the twentieth century. In 1994, the increase in bald eagle numbers even prompted the United States to downgrade it from "endangered" to "threatened" status on the endangered species list. However, the eagle is not completely out of danger.

Though an increase in bald eagle numbers to five thousand nesting pairs has caused the U.S. government to

Book Silent Spring Captures Attention

In 1962, a U.S. biologist named Rachel Carson wrote a book about the dangers of pesticide use called *Silent Spring*. In it, Carson made this startling proclamation about the implications of pesticide use for the future of all life on the planet earth:

> Synthetic pesticides have been so thoroughly distributed throughout the animate and inanimate world that they occur virtually everywhere. They have been recovered from most of the major river systems and even from streams of groundwater flowing unseen through the earth. . . . Residue of these chemicals linger in our soil to which they have been applied a dozen years before. They have entered and lodged in the bodies of fish, birds, reptiles, and domestic and wild animals so universally that scientists carrying on animal experimentation find it almost impossible to locate subjects free from such contamination.

Until the time of the book's publication, only scientists and researchers had been aware of what pesticides could do, but then the general public had the opportunity to understand the problems posed by these very powerful chemicals. Concern grew and a serious discussion about the effects of pesticides began.

Biologist Rachel Carson brought early attention to the environmental risks posed by pesticides.

Although the bald eagle population has increased in recent years, residue of DDT can still be found in some of the young.

consider removing it entirely from the endangered species list, an argument can still be made that the decision is premature. Early recovery efforts did not anticipate the continued battle against the long-lasting presence and effects of DDT and dichloro-diphenyl-ethylene (DDE), the chemical produced by the breakdown of DDT, in the environment. DDE has a half-life of 57.6 years. Half-life means the length of time necessary for half of a given quantity of the substance to break down into less harmful components. Because of this long half-life, significant amounts of DDE linger in the soil, in the bodies of the prey bald eagles eat, and in the nation's waterways. Even in the late 1980s, some bald eagles released from recovery programs still were not effectively laying and hatching eggs, evidence of continued contamination of the environment by chlorinated hydrocarbons. Though recovery programs can supplement food and provide temporary housing for bald eagles, they cannot address the problems these residual amounts of the pesticides still cause with the birds' reproductive systems. One of the signs of a complete recovery is a species' ability to reproduce in the wild without any assistance from humans, and until bald eagles can manage to reproduce on their own, they cannot be truly considered out of danger.

Also, legal alternative pesticides to DDT still harm bald eagles, even when the people who use them follow strict application guidelines. As *Audubon* magazine writer Ted Williams says,

For years conventional wisdom . . . had it that at least raptors could resist lethal poisoning when organophosphates or carbamate pesticides were "properly" applied. But that superstition was debunked in 1985, when the deaths of bald eagles were traced to the carbamate carbofuran. . . . Discoveries have shown that about 40 pesticides, the bulk of them still registered in the United States, can kill birds even when used according to the directions on the label.[10]

For example, the pesticide phorate was applied to a field near a South Dakota wetland at only a partial dosage in the winter, but the following spring researchers found hundreds of dead waterfowl there and many carcasses of bald eagles that had scavenged these contaminated birds.

Peregrine numbers decrease

Another well-known victim of DDT and DDE, the peregrine falcon, saw its populations sharply decline worldwide during the middle part of the twentieth century. For example, in the United States, a 1930–40 survey of eastern peregrine populations counted 275 eyries used by the birds, but by 1964, the survey showed not a single one was still used by a peregrine breeding pair. Due in large part to use of chlorinated hydrocarbon pesticides in the United States, the peregrine was virtually eliminated from the country by 1968, except in the extreme north and parts of the west. Similarly, in Great Britain and the rest of Europe, populations declined rapidly throughout the 1960s and 1970s.

Just as bald eagles had trouble reproducing and raising healthy young when DDT and its lingering form DDE had entered their systems, so did peregrine falcons. High levels of contamination not only thinned peregrine eggshells but also caused an abnormally large number of peregrine females and an abnormally small number of males in each clutch of eggs. This imbalance decreased the available number of breeding pairs since there were not enough males to breed with peregrine females. DDE contamination also caused a problem called "embryo feminization" in which male peregrines were born with female sex organs and thus were unable to reproduce. DDE also caused the peregrine falcon's estrogen levels to rise high enough

Some populations of peregrine falcons still suffer from the lingering effects of pesticides.

to cause cancer of the breast and testicles and low sperm counts. Scientists also noted that DDE-affected peregrines mated less and appeared more stressed than those not affected by the chemical.

Peregrine falcons recovered?

With the banning of U.S. domestic uses of DDT in 1972, the peregrine falcon began a gradual but significant recovery throughout North America. The joint U.S.-Canadian recovery goal for the peregrine was to reestablish 631 breeding pairs. As of 1998, the number of breeding pairs totaled 1,593. Many of the birds live in large metropolitan areas such as Seattle and New York City.

Though the peregrine falcon, like the bald eagle, has rallied in response to discontinued use of DDT and DDE in many countries, some research and observation of the birds in the wild indicates that the battle against these pesticides has not yet been won. Like bald eagles, peregrines still eat prey contaminated by significant amounts of chlorinated hydrocarbons that persist in the soil and water supply.

Significant amounts of chlorinated hydrocarbons dumped into the the world's oceans and waterways still linger there and are eaten by creatures such as shellfish, thus entering the peregrine's food chain. For years chemical companies daily funneled hundreds of pounds of DDE into the ocean near Los Angeles, California. Peregrine expert Galen Rowell says, "DDT residue contamination of the ocean floor still measures more than 300 parts per million—making this area the world's worst DDT hot spot."[11] Rowell's research shows that the lingering effects of organophosphates on the bird's reproductive system are still serious, especially in coastal areas. For example, female peregrines still significantly outnumber males along the East Coast of the United States.

Lee Aulman, a biologist tracking the health of the California peregrine population, is concerned rather than encouraged when he looks at the increased numbers of peregrines now living in the wild because they give people an incorrect idea of the peregrine's recovery. According to Aulman, a disproportionate number of the birds he sees are those released from captive breeding programs. To see a clearer picture of the peregrine's hope for survival in a land still contaminated with pesticides, Aulman indicates people must look at the nesting and brooding success of those reintroduced to the wild: "All the words, numbers, and graphs in the world won't tell the story of what's happening on these wild sea cliffs. There's such a big difference between reading that 60 percent of the eggs we collected last year didn't hatch and the incredibly sad reality of seeing a pair of these magnificent creatures aggressively defending a clutch of dead eggs."[12]

Pesticide alternatives to chlorinated hydrocarbons also can cause peregrine reproductive problems. Recently, for example, researchers found that a widely used derivative of DDT called dicofol causes captive peregrines to experience eggshell thinning, behavioral stress, and impairment of the instinctive aggressiveness needed for hunting and for defending a nest. Some evidence suggests that alternative pesticides may even cause the peregrine to lay eggs that will never hatch. According to Galen Rowell, a healthy peregrine pair normally hatches four eggs per clutch. Many peregrines reintroduced to coastal areas now raise only one egg, and then only if they do not crush a thin-shelled egg during brooding. Rowell and other researchers following the east and west coast U.S. peregrine population fear low numbers cannot sustain a genetically healthy population, because formerly only the fastest and best hunters of the clutch lived to pass on their genetic makeup. With only one chick per nest, even relatively weak birds will live to breed and raise similarly weak offspring.

Migration and pesticides

Even though certain pesticides may be banned in the United States, these chemicals sometimes find their way back to this country, carried in the tissues of migratory birds that spend part of every year in countries where the substances are still in use. For example, another reason pesticides still endanger the peregrine falcon is that the U.S. population preys on birds that migrate to Latin America, where DDT is still widely used. This means the peregrine faces essentially the same dangers it did before the pesticide was banned in its home country.

The Swainson's hawk became a victim of pesticides mostly because of its migratory habits.

Swainson's hawk endangered

Contaminated prey is not the only thing that migrates. Sometimes, the raptors themselves are migratory and fly into areas where dangerous pesticides are used. Migration causes problems for the Swainson's hawk, a raptor that migrates seasonally from its winter home in the plains of the United States and Canada to its winter home in the pampas of South America. About ten years ago, when Argentinean farmers began to grow moneymaking crops such as sunflowers, corn, and soybeans, they also began to use monocrotophos, a pesticide used to control the grasshoppers that fed heavily on those crops. Monocrotophos had already been banned in the United States because of its toxicity. Even trace amounts of the chemical can kill a bird the size of a Swainson's hawk.

About the time Argentinean farmers began spraying monocrotophos on their crops, an American researcher, Brian Woodbridge, noticed a markedly decreasing number of Swainson's hawks returning to spend the summer in the United States. He decided to investigate. With satellite telemetry devices, Woodbridge tracked two migrating Swainson's hawks to the pampas of Argentina. He learned that Swainson's hawks, which the Argentineans call *aguilucho langostero* or the hawk that eats locusts, fed almost exclusively on grasshoppers, the very insect targeted by monocrotophos.

When the Argentinean farmers sprayed their fields with monocrotophos, the hawks became poisoned by the pesticide. Monocrotophos has the same effects as a nerve gas— it interferes with nerve transmission and causes shut-down of the respiratory system. Some hawks died after eating and digesting grasshoppers killed by monocrotophos. Many more, however, were killed by coming in direct contact with the spray of the pesticide. Naturalist Les Line explains, "Woodbridge says it's a common sight to see a flock of Swainson's hawks spiraling down to earth at the first sight of a tractor stirring up clouds of grasshoppers from a field. The tractor . . . could well be towing a spray rig filled with monocrotophos."[13] In just one season, twenty thousand Swainson's hawks, a number equaling about 5 percent of its population, died from respiratory failure brought on by monocrotophos poisoning.

Fight to save the Swainson's

Though steps have been taken to keep monocrotophos from harming the Swainson's hawks, the birds are still in danger. The Argentinean government has banned use of monocrotophos on alfalfa and sunflower fields, but the municipal governments of smaller villages have trouble coming up with the money and staff to enforce this federal ban on the pesticide. Also, thirty chemical companies continue to produce monocrotophos and make it available because it is relatively inexpensive and easy to make. Says Woodbridge, "Don't blame the farmers . . . the problem lies with an international marketing system that supplies them with inappropriate chemicals and doesn't give them the kind of information they need to make the right choices."[14]

In such situations, it takes coordinated efforts to help the endangered raptors, and there are many participants in the fight to save the Swainson's hawk. Working together with the American Bird Conservancy, Novartis, a chemical company that formerly produced 20 percent of the world's supply of monocrotophos, announced it would no longer make the pesticide. The company also agreed to buy back unused supplies of the chemical from farmers as part of the pact with the Bird Conservancy.

Informed Argentinean farmers too have played a crucial role in educating their fellow farmers about the danger of the pesticide. One soybean farmer, Augustin Lanusse, "drove his pickup for six days around his and neighboring farms, tallying dead birds and talking with farmers about the hawk kill and what could be done about it."[15] For the most part, Argentinean farmers are disturbed by the bird kills and want to know what they can do to protect both their crops and the hawks.

Continued pesticide use

Nations such as Argentina contribute to only part of the pesticide problem facing birds of prey. The United States has stricter regulations about domestic uses of pesticides and more information about the effects of the chemicals on both humans and animals than many nations do. U.S. companies still produce and export the bulk of the world's pesticides, however. Writer Les Line observes:

After analyzing U.S. Customs shipping records, the Los Angeles-based Foundation for Advancements in Science Education . . . reported this past spring that at least 344 million pounds of hazardous pesticides were known to have left U.S. ports from 1992 through 1994. The category includes chemicals that have been banned or se-

American companies make and export some hazardous pesticides that have been banned in this country.

verely restricted by the U.S. Environmental Protection Agency and products like monocrotophos whose domestic use has been discontinued.[16]

Another obstacle to addressing the dangers of pesticides to birds of prey is that few countries have national procedures for collecting, receiving, and processing data about those birds that are killed by them. Even in the United States, where such procedures are in place, reliable data are hard to obtain. For example, to convince the U.S. Environmental Protection Agency to remove pesticides from the market, the Fish and Wildlife Service must produce high bird body counts, which would help pinpoint deaths to raptors as well. However, before Fish and Wildlife Service officials can count the number of dead birds by walking, driving, or flying over an affected area, the carcasses have often been scavenged by humans interested in trophy gathering and by birds of prey, that will sicken or die as a result of eating the contaminated birds. To teach people just how difficult tracking bird deaths related to pesticides can be, the Fish and Wildlife Service arranged for a Bird Mortality Workshop at the Patuxent Wildlife Research Center in Laurel, Maryland. Workshop participants fanned out over farmland where officials had scattered eighty bird carcasses a day earlier. When participants had thoroughly scanned the area, they found only a fraction of the dead birds.

The continuing threat from pesticides, however, is just one of many faced by birds of prey. Unlike pesticide application, many human activities have a less direct but equally damaging effect on bird of prey populations worldwide. As huge human populations grow in many countries, the need for food, shelter, and transportation increases as well. Many raptor species have declined as a direct result of such struggles over resources.

3

The Struggle for Space and Resources

BY MEETING THEIR increasing needs for food, shelter, and transportation, people around the world inevitably endanger birds of prey. As British ornithologist James Ferguson-Lees says "galloping habitat destruction . . . affects countless forms of animal life that then have to compete for ever-decreasing and often more disturbed remnants of the habitats to which they are adapted."[17] Human settlements now exist where birds of prey formerly ranged. In most cases, raptors cannot and will not live in close proximity to humans. When humans move into raptor habitat, some of the birds are inevitably displaced.

Even if people do not build their houses in a raptor's habitat, they often need to use it for other purposes. For example, raptor habitat is burned and plowed to clear more land for growing crops, and raptor species' natural prey populations can be driven out so humans can use land for grazing livestock. Also, loggers cut down forests essential to many tree-dwelling raptors and to the prey they feed upon. People carve transportation corridors for roads, railways, and airports through raptor habitat, reducing the size of the birds' territories and killing off or displacing their prey populations in the process.

People harm birds of prey in more direct ways as well. Again, limited resources are at the heart of the conflict. In some cases, people who make their living directly from the land or who hunt the same prey as raptors believe the birds

Losers in the War over Resources

Though people can live closer to each other than birds of prey and better adapt to changing resources, they have not entirely conquered their territorial natures. Unfortunately, human conflicts, large or small, cannot help but devastate raptor populations. For example, the Congo Bay owl, which was once thought extinct, was recently located in the Itombwe forest of Zaire, Africa. Unfortunately, the owl lived in an area between Burundi and Rwanda, where farmers and cattle herders clashed with each other over use of the land.

Not only has the frequent fighting between herdsmen and farmers made the owl's habitat a dangerous place to live, a corn blight caused the farmers to cut and clear huge areas of rain forest habitat the owl needs to survive.

The *New York Times* quoted John Hart, senior conservation geologist with the Wildlife Conservation Society, as saying, "How do you protect the Itombwe? . . . What about the people living there? It is difficult to find a strategy to insure the conservation of an area of such importance for biological diversity, while improving resources for people." The Itombwe owl's future, like the future of the area, is not bright.

are competitors and shoot, poison, or trap them. Sometimes people even kill birds of prey for food.

The bald eagle's troubles

Little more than a century after the founding of the United States, a few people began officially recording bald eagle sightings. They found that the bird's populations had begun to shrink. One factor may have been competition for limited food supplies. For example, salmon fishermen in Alaska disliked eagles because they depended on the same food supply and fished the same waters. Between 1917 and 1954, the territory of Alaska offered a bounty of two dollars for each eagle carcass turned in by hunters. Before the bounty was lifted, 128,000 eagles had been killed.

Eagles are killed primarily because farmers view them as a threat to their livestock and a competitor for natural resources.

Throughout the middle part of this century, the bald eagle's story was one of steady decline. In 1940, the Bald Eagle Protection Act made it illegal to kill a bald eagle because its numbers had dropped dramatically. In 1978, the bald eagle was added to the U.S. Endangered Species List. Killing an animal protected under the U.S. Endangered Species Act is a federal crime and can mean imprisonment for the offender.

Despite legal protection, eagle poisoning is still common on the sheep ranches of the western United States because ranchers view them as predators that threaten domestic herds. In his book *Eagle's Plume*, writer Bruce Beans says that even though records of the Agriculture Statistics Board revealed that eagles did indeed feed on sheep, these statistics also revealed that they could be blamed for just 1.5 percent of total sheep losses. Beans goes on to say that "that hardly justifies placing poisoned carcasses on the open range where they are clearly visible to sharp-eyed raptors."[18]

Efforts to reassure ranchers that bald eagles have a minimal effect on their herds have been largely unsuccessful. Eagles and their protectors still seem to some ranchers a real threat to their way of life. When a rancher comes upon an eagle feeding on a young lamb, he may not think about whether the bird actually killed the creature or not. Many ranchers simply feel a need to protect their herd. Moreover, some ranchers see themselves as under attack. Beans quotes one man convicted of poisoning eagles as saying, "We've got people in this country who don't want any animals killed. . . . They're more interested about animal life than human life. They want to make the western states one big wildlife refuge, want to raise coyotes and wolves. . . . We're here, too. I violated the law and I admit it, but in my own mind I figured I was justified in trying to protect myself."[19]

The recent dramatic increase in bald eagle numbers nationwide does not mean the species is out of danger everywhere. As naturalist Les Line reports, "Bald eagles avoid human company, and scientists warn that, despite the recent upturn in their numbers, the species is unlikely to adapt to human intrusion. This means that there will be little room for eagles in areas like northern Chesapeake Bay because of accelerating housing and recreational development."[20]

Human intrusion into bald eagle habitat does not always take the form of roads or buildings. For example, in Florida recently, Sanford-Orlando Airport officials cut down a bald eagle nesting tree near the airport because they believed the birds would crash into airplanes in the area. They did this in response to new guidelines from the Federal Aviation Administration that call for creating buffer areas "between airports and 'wildlife attractants' such as wetlands and roosting habitats."[21]

Grey eagle-buzzard poisoned

Sometimes, a raptor is not directly targeted but gets caught in the conflict between humans and another species. For example, the grey eagle-buzzard of Argentina, an important link in the country's food chain, drew the attention of conservationists when its population numbers began to drop. Investigation into the problem revealed that the bird was eating the remains of predators that were being poisoned with strychnine by Argentinean farmers who wanted to control what they saw as threats to livestock.

In response, environmental educators are attempting to teach local farmers that without the gray eagle-buzzard and other predators, they will have difficulty controlling the nonnative European rabbits and hares that destroy local crops and pastures.

Cape vulture endangered

Sometimes the mere perception that a particular species of raptor is a competitor with humans is enough to land it in trouble. The cape vulture of South Africa faces a number of problems because of its proximity to ranching communities. Because the bird's range includes a wide variety of terrain, including mountains, open plains, hills, and gorges, they are highly visible to ranchers, who have been known to shoot the birds when they see them feeding on the carcasses of dead livestock. Such instances are on the rise. Where once the cape vultures fed on wild animals that grazed in the area, they now depend on the food provided by carcasses of the domestic livestock which have displaced these wild animals.

Furthermore, the very dependence of the vultures on dead livestock is leading to their decline. Ranchers have begun removing the carcasses of dead livestock because they fear the spread of disease to other livestock. This has further reduced the cape vulture's access to calcium available in the bones of the carcasses. Their calcium-deficient diet has left cape vulture chicks with deformed legs and wings.

Conservationists in South Africa are trying to protect the endangered cape vulture by both dispelling myths about the innate evil of vultures and by showing local people their value in the environment. They have established feeding areas where cape vultures can eat both the meat and bones of livestock carcasses. The feeding grounds have provided an opportunity for the public to learn about the birds and their nutritional needs. Conservationists have tried to teach local people about the unique and useful role vultures play as disease controllers since their digestive systems destroy bacteria found in the carcasses of diseased animals.

Sea eagle numbers fall

One raptor, the sea eagle of Europe, is representative of the range of threats faced by birds of prey due to the variety of harassment it faces. In the late nineteenth century, many European countries established bounties on sea eagles because the fishermen feared that they fed too heavily on commercial fish stocks. In addition, sea eagles nest in accessible locations, making them particularly vulnerable to egg collectors. Even earlier, sea eagles in Britain were in trouble.

To create solid ground for farming and human habitations, fens—vast lowland areas covered by water that the sea eagle depended on for habitat and food—were being drained. By the late eighteenth century, sea eagle numbers in Britain were already in serious decline.

Steller's Sea Eagle: The Next Endangered Raptor?

Though not yet officially endangered, the Steller's sea eagle suffers population losses each year from increasing habitat destruction. Like the bald eagle, the Steller's sea eagle must live along the shorelines where it can eat sockeye salmon. Even though the eagle hunts in sparsely populated areas of Siberia (northern Russia) near the Bering Sea, its habitat of ancient forest is slowly being cut down to make way for housing developments and industrial complexes.

Scotland's hen harriers decline

Sometimes birds of prey find themselves in direct competition with other hunters. Hen harriers, a bird hawk, and hunters in Scotland are in just such a face-off over grouse, a small game bird. Members of the Scottish Landowner's Federation favor legalized killing of the harriers because they are concerned that the hawks will deplete populations of grouse, affecting recreational hunting in the area. The hen harrier, whose primary prey is the grouse, is now threatened in Scotland because so many have been killed and their nests destroyed. Rob Edwards, a writer for *New Scientist* magazine writes that "researchers found footprints, litter and cigarette butts around hen harrier nests, suggesting interference. Evidence that harriers had been killed included empty gun cartridges and the remains of traps."[22] Edwards goes on to note that game keepers targeted breeding female hen harriers to prevent successful population growth. A study conducted by the Royal Society for the Protection of Birds revealed that the hen harrier population has been so depleted that the birds are not able to reproduce enough to sustain a population large enough to maintain genetic diversity and the overall health of the species.

Northern spotted owl makes headlines

Even when humans have no direct reason to dislike birds of prey, incompatible needs can lead to problems. In such cases, the birds often lose. The controversy surrounding the threatened northern spotted owl represents one of the most famous examples of a raptor's struggle with humans for space and resources. The problem centers around 3 million acres of old-growth forest in the Pacific Northwest region of the United States and the small owl who depends on this unique habitat to survive. Though the northern spotted owl alone obviously did not cause the argument between forest industry officials and environmentalists, it did draw national attention to it.

For habitat, northern spotted owls require old-growth forests—that is, ancient forests of hemlocks, redwood, and Douglas fir that have never been cut. Some trees in the northern spotted owl's habitat are as old as two thousand years. Old-growth forests provide suitable habitat in a number of ways that younger forests cannot. The understory, or lower level of older trees, provides the owls with shelter from the sun in summer. The tops of the oldest trees allow the owls to roost in the sun for warmth in winter. The

Mexican Spotted Owl Habitat Threatened

The Mexican spotted owl is closely related to the northern spotted owl and is also threatened by logging of old-growth forests, but in the southwestern United States. In 1993 the bird was added to the Endangered Species List as a threatened species. Mexican spotted owls require a forest with trees of different sizes to survive. Forestry officials have argued that because in old-growth forests trees grow so close together insects easily establish themselves and attack whole stands of trees, and fires more easily spread and are difficult to fight.

Conservationists are skeptical that forestry management plans will protect the Mexican spotted owl in Utah, Colorado, Arizona, and New Mexico. The plans call for creating buffer zones of six hundred acres around known nesting sites where no forest can be logged. The plans also say that logging companies must leave trees standing in areas where the birds might live even if they are not known to live there. However, they also call for what *Science News* writer Tina Adler calls "slightly less dense stands than the government's new prescription, so both loggers and owls can use the same land." Environmentalists say there is not enough proof that the owls will adapt to such conditions and insist that the timber industry must address the needs of the remaining two thousand Mexican owl breeding pairs for dense forests with trees of mixed height.

thick protection of old trees also keeps the snow off the ground so that the owls can more easily see and catch their prey. Furthermore, as ancient trees eventually decay, they provide a crucial nesting habitat of holes and crevices for the owls.

Unfortunately, these same old-growth forests contain trees that are particularly desirable to humans for use as building materials. The region's logging industry has long depended on the availability of old-growth stands of trees to cut, but the loss of old-growth forest means that fewer and fewer owls have the habitat they need for survival. In arguing for logging restrictions, environmentalists have had to face the moral issue of whether protecting the owl's habitat, may cause people to lose their jobs.

The debate over the owls' fate has caused extraordinary anger and anxiety. At the center of the debate has been whether to add the northern spotted owl to the Endangered Species List. In 1990, the U.S. Fish and Wildlife Service added the bird to the list as a threatened species. However, since the owl's status was listed as simply threatened rather than endangered, logging went on as usual.

After years of discussion between environmentalists, the timber industry, and government agencies, the groups have reached a compromise. Logging has finally been restricted in areas known to contain nesting northern spotted owls, and large sections of old-growth forest have been preserved for owl habitat.

The northern spotted owl is not entirely out of danger, however. Logging of the owl's dense forest habitat has made it possible for the eastern barred owl, a relative of the spotted owl, to become established in areas where previously only spotted owls lived. The barred owl is more adaptive to habitat changes than the northern spotted owl and is also a more aggressive hunter and nester. Biologists who have studied the two owls say that in cases where the barred owl and northern spotted owl habitat overlaps, the barred owl usually wins out.

Harpy eagles hunted

Other raptors are less threatened by logging than by direct attack by humans. Though the threatened harpy eagle suffers from significant logging of its rain forest habitat in Central and South America, the biggest threat to its survival is hunting by humans. Wild bird traders in the area believe that by preying on macaws, a kind of parrot, harpy eagles directly threaten their livelihood. Neil Rettig, a naturalist who studied the harpy eagle in Guyana, says, "Even though the colorful parrots make up only a small percentage of the eagles' diet, trappers who sell macaws to the pet trade (getting only two dollars a bird) sometimes kill harpy eagles, viewing them as competitors."[23] The large eagles are themselves also sought after by people for their

The harpy eagle is hunted by those who export exotic parrots because the eagle's diet includes the colorful macaw parrot, which often brings a high price.

meat. Some people even kill the harpy eagle for its feathers and other body parts, believing they possess special power to protect those who carry them.

Philippine eagle habitat destroyed

For some birds of prey, the complete loss of their habitat appears imminent. One of the world's twenty most endangered raptors, the Philippine eagle, faces near complete destruction of its unique forest habitat. Despite the fact that it is the Filipino national symbol, fewer than two hundred birds remain in the Philippines. The birds roost atop large and uniquely sturdy plants called epiphytic ferns that grow without soil, drawing nutrients from the air and rain and securing themselves to the rain forest canopy. Says naturalist Les Line, "According to one grim prediction, the Philippines by 2007 could be virtually denuded of both old- and second-growth forest, and presumably divested of eagles because of legal and illegal logging, slash-and-burn farming, charcoal making and firewood gathering."[24] Now less than four thousand square miles of old-growth forest remain in the country.

The troubled status of the Philippine eagle has been known for some time. As early as the 1960s, conservationists from the Philippines and abroad fought to save the Philippine eagle. Though the Filipino legislature passed laws in the 1970s to establish sanctuaries for the birds and to prohibit killing or capturing them, this legislation was never enforced. Moreover, the information put out by conservationists mainly reached city dwellers who had little contact with the birds and minimal reason for concern about their habitat. Those who live in the forest have continued to log the eagle's habitat heavily. When efforts to preserve the forests first got underway, many Filipinos felt strongly opposed because they feared it could affect their export of wood products. Those who live near the forest and use its trees "consider it an inexhaustible resource."[25]

The speed with which the Philippines have lost old-growth forests is astonishing. Karen Puracan, a conservationist now fighting to save the Philippine eagle, describes

The Lone Eagle Gets Involved

In 1969, Charles Lindbergh, the famous American aviator, donated a captive Philippine eagle to the Philippine Parks and Wildlife Commission in the hope that measures would be put into place to protect the severely endangered bird. Though not the first person to express concern over the bird's plight, Lindbergh's fame helped add urgency and credibility to the conservation efforts to save the Philippine eagle. Had it not been for Lindbergh's interest in saving the bird, the Philippine government may not have been as quick to prohibit the formerly widespread killing, trapping, and nest disturbance that had weakened the population or to set aside habitat sanctuaries.

the effect logging has had on the bird's habitat, saying "Originally 94% of the Philippines was covered in lush tropical rain forests. After World War II, this fell to 40%. Current estimates place the figures at 25% (some say even 18%). This represents a 55% loss from 1950 to 1991 . . . only 41 years. Rain forests continue to be cut at the astonishing rate of 170,000 hectares a year ."[26] The eagle's situation is extremely precarious, and some biologists fear that the Philippine eagles will not survive because they will not have enough suitable habitat. Each mating pair requires about thirty-six square miles of forest habitat.

Spanish imperial eagle nears extinction

The loss of habitat may be rapid or happen over many generations, but the end result for affected raptors is the same. Like the Philippine eagle, the Spanish imperial eagle is one of the world's most endangered raptors and suffers mostly from habitat loss. Only 150 breeding pairs remain in the wild. Though the imperial eagle ranges from central Asia to Spain, its Spanish population is the most endangered.

In the past, Mediterranean forests like those in Spain were made up mainly of oak trees that for years remained virtually undisturbed. In these thick forests, the Spanish eagle preyed on an abundance of rabbits and other small prey. But over the last century, these cork oak forests have been cut down and replanted with faster growing pine and eucalyptus trees that are more commercially valuable. With the loss of the cork oak trees came the loss of the Spanish eagle's prey and its habitat.

The Spanish imperial eagle faces other dangers as well. Biologists recently discovered that the power lines that enclose one of the birds' last refuges, Doñana National Park, have been electrocuting some of the eagles. When they perch on pylons atop electric poles, female Spanish imperial eagles, which are larger than males, are likely to touch live wires on either side. Unfortunately, if a species is to have any chance of recovery, a strong population of females is crucial. Electrocution has already taken its toll on the small population of females.

Also, though natural to the bird, fratricide (killing of siblings) among eaglets reduces their chances of recovery since their numbers are already on the decline. The future of the species now depends on biologists' attempts to remove

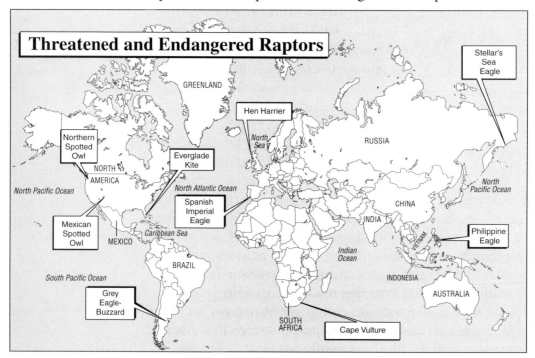

weaker eaglets likely to be killed by their siblings and place them in nests of parents with fewer young. This solution is less than ideal, however, since the long-term health of a species is not helped by preserving the weakest individuals.

Wetland drainage endangers kite

Even when a bird's habitat does not appear grossly affected by humans, interference with only a small aspect of the habitat can be devastating. The Everglade kite, a raptor that lives primarily in south Florida, came close to extinction as a direct result of habitat alteration. People drained excessive amounts of its marsh habitat for agricultural, residential, and commercial development. Frequent manipulation of the water levels in the area nearly wiped out the supply of the bird's primary prey, the apple snail, and in turn nearly wiped it out as well.

Ironically, human manipulation of its habitat again may be the only thing that can save the Everglade kite from extinction. Under normal conditions, kite nests are too flimsy to stand up in strong storms, and the greatly reduced population cannot withstand the loss of nests even to causes that naturally occur in the wild. However, since biologists began building artificial nests, a small population of birds has gradually recovered around the Lake Okeechobee region of south Florida.

Condor victim of habitat disturbance

Of course, in many cases, no one type of human activity is to blame for a species' decline, but the sum total of interference takes a heavy toll. In little more than a century, human activity caused the California condor's numbers to drop significantly. For example, in the early 1900s, human encroachment into the California condor's habitat and hunting ground greatly reduced its population and territory. Like the bald eagle, California condors have great difficulty nesting and breeding in close proximity to humans. California condor egg collecting was a popular hobby in the nineteenth and early twentieth centuries that affected the success of the bird's breeding.

Cattle and sheep ranching also took their toll on the California condor. In the first half of the twentieth century, the birds died from eating poisoned carcasses left as part of a predator control program designed to control populations of coyotes, bobcats, and other large mammals believed to be killing livestock. Ironically, because humans removed so many native mammal species in the California condor's territory, ranches became crucial to the survival of the condor, because the birds could still feed on the carcasses of dead livestock.

In the second half of the twentieth century, even the ranch land became attractive as residential and commercial property, which further reduced available food for condors. By the 1970s, the once huge range of California condors had been cornered into California's San Joaquin Valley, an area of rain-carved valleys and gorges.

In the case of these large vultures, conservationists believed that merely preserving and protecting habitat would be insufficient to save the raptor. They needed to attempt a radical technique called "captive breeding and reintroduction" if the species was to survive at all.

4

Captive Breeding and Reintroduction

SOMETIMES, THE DAMAGE done to raptor populations has proved so severe that merely preserving remaining habitat is not enough to allow a species to recover. In such cases, though, it is sometimes possible to reverse the damage with a radical form of intervention called captive breeding and reintroduction. Biologists began to consider such intervention in the mid-1960s when conservationists in many countries classified particular raptor species as endangered because of their dwindling populations.

As is true with many untested and radical techniques, opinions varied widely about whether captive breeding and reintroduction into the environment would be a good idea. Some believed that even though they had little proof that raptors like the endangered California condor would breed successfully in captivity, reintroduction was worth a try if it could save the bird from extinction. On the other hand, opponents argued that if a species could no longer adapt to changes in its environment, it should be allowed to become extinct. Proponents of reintroduction countered that though extinction is indeed a natural process, the rate of extinction for many species including the California condor had been increasing at an unnatural rate because of human activity. Ultimately, people decided to try captive breeding and reintroduction in the hope that the species could be saved.

Habitat concerns

One of the first concerns in a captive-breeding and reintroduction program is to determine where the birds will eventually be reintroduced to the wild. Reintroduced birds need suitable nest sites, adequate food supplies, and enough territory for the reintroduced population to reestablish itself.

Some conservationists suggest that rather than funnel resources only into saving an endangered raptor in one area of a country, funds should also be spent working with the country to preserve the entire ecosystem so that the birds have a place where they can sustain their populations in the wild. For example, conservationists trying to breed the Philippine eagle in captivity know that without a change in attitude in the local residents, the bird cannot survive in the wild. Local foresters continue to strip the eagle's forested

Members of the Peregrine Falcon Project attempt to help a falcon fly after an unsuccessful first attempt.

home because, with the birds considered to be safe in captivity, they believe continued logging of their habitat is no longer a problem.

In some cases, though a raptor's habitat may have changed radically, it can still be reintroduced if suitable nesting areas and prey populations exist. When biologists discovered that the eastern U.S. population of the peregrine falcon, which had become extinct, could build nests on buildings, they saw many potential eastern release sites. For peregrine falcons, the skyscrapers of urban areas in the eastern United States provided just as many nest sites as their preferred habitat of cliffs and rocky outcrops. Also, cities provided an abundant source of one of the peregrine falcon's favorite foods—pigeons.

Scientists interested in the captive breeding and reintroduction of the harpy eagle to Panama had to determine if the designated area for reintroduction, Soberania National Park, would have sufficient habitat to sustain a reintroduced population. Before the captive-breeding program began, biologists carefully monitored the existing breeding pairs in a similar area to see if they still had enough nesting areas and food resources.

Capturing endangered raptors from the wild

To begin captive breeding and reintroduction of an endangered raptor, healthy individuals of a species must first be removed from the wild and brought to a captive-breeding facility. By breeding endangered raptors in a controlled environment, biologists can protect them from further danger or human interference.

One of the first birds removed from the wild for captive breeding was the Mauritius kestrel. The bird had declined for a number of reasons: DDT contamination, persecution by humans who believed them to be chicken hunters, and destruction of their forest habitats by nonnative plants brought to the island of Mauritius by European settlers in the 1500s. When the wild population of the kestrels had dwindled to just six birds—so few that if one member died, the species could die out—biologists removed several individuals from the wild to a captive-breeding facility. The offspring of those individual kestrels initially captured from the wild today inhabit the island of Mauritius.

Facing a similar situation, the Condor Recovery Team resorted to capturing California condors from the wild when they realized the birds were not reproducing fast enough to ensure the survival of the species. Throughout the early 1980s, the team set out animal carcasses and threw nets over the birds when they began to feed.

The birds were then transported to captive-breeding facilities in the San Diego Wild Animal Park and the Los Angeles Zoo, where scientists had built flight pens, sterile food preparation areas, and incubation rooms. Netted flight pens were carefully constructed to accommodate the condors' massive size and need for exercise. Nesting areas and incubation areas were designed with curtains and other visual barriers so that human caretakers would be able to observe the condors without the birds seeing them.

Each wild condor was crated and quickly transported to the captive-breeding facility for initial observation and then left alone for the first few days until it could adjust to its new surroundings. Gradually, the wild condors were removed from the San Joaquin Valley and placed in the captive-breeding facilities. In 1987, the last remaining California condor was removed from the wild by Audubon Society biologists working in conjunction with the Condor Recovery Team.

Throughout this period, those condors remaining in the wild were also enlisted in the recovery effort. Condor Recovery Team members removed eggs from wild condor nests to be incubated where they would be safe from predators and human interference. As with many raptor species, the California condor lays a second and sometimes a third egg in a breeding season if an egg disappears or fails to hatch.

Members of the Condor Recovery Team release a condor on the Vermillion Cliffs in Northern Arizona.

Program Critics

In 1983, at the height of the arguments over whether to attempt captive breeding of the California condor, Kenneth Brower, critic of the program, believed that removing the birds from the wild and raising them in captivity did not address problems the birds would face in a habitat inhospitable to them. He believed the breeding program addressed only a symptom of the condor's problem, not the cause. The views he expressed in an *Atlantic Monthly* article, "The Naked Vulture and the Thinking Ape," are still heard today: "Captive breeding threatens the condor indirectly, by diverting attention and funds from the bird's true problems and from components of the larger problem aimed at solving these problems. . . . the captive-breeding program has preempted funds for acquisition of crucial lands, for hunter education, for law enforcement, and for poison studies."

Volunteers needed

Sometimes, of course, a population of raptors has been wiped out in a given area, even though the habitat remains suitable for the birds. To reintroduce an endangered raptor to an area where it has become extinct, individuals of the species must be taken from healthy populations in a different geographic area and held for captive breeding. In the eastern United States, by the late 1950s peregrine falcons had been wiped out by the effects of DDT. Peregrines were brought from healthy populations in Alaska to Cornell University in New York, where scientists bred them in captivity. Descendants of this initial group of Alaskan peregrines were then reintroduced to Minneapolis, Minnesota. Twelve birds were, in turn, brought from Minneapolis to Rochester, New York, to establish a population there.

A member of the Rochester Peregrine Falcon Project holds a peregrine chick.

Once captured, wild birds must be treated with the utmost care. The stress of being handled by humans can be deadly. Researchers on the Condor Recovery Team learned a hard lesson about the stressful effects human handling can have on wild raptors targeted for captive breeding. Early in the condor recovery program, a condor chick died while biologists tried to measure it to gather evidence that the parents were not able to care for it adequately in the wild. Kenneth Brower, writer for the *Atlantic Monthly* said, "Autopsy revealed that the chick had been in perfect health—weight normal, no parasites or pesticide. It had been killed by the stress of handling."[27] After this initial accident, condor recovery team members rarely handled condor chicks, and when they absolutely had to, they took care that the birds would not see their human caretakers.

Danger of disease

Captive raptors are also susceptible to diseases they would not have been exposed to in the wild, and special care must be taken to prevent their exposure. For example, some captive Mauritius kestrels contracted human diseases, such as hepatitis, from contact with their human caretakers.

Financing Captive Breeding

One of the first steps to breeding and raising raptors in captivity is gathering the money necessary to carry out the project. Some endangered raptors have been captive-bred in facilities with staff paid for by corporations with an interest in restoring the natural environment. For example, money for captive breeding of the harpy eagle of Panama came from FedEx, Exxon, and Disney.

The Rochester Gas and Electric Company of New York provided funding and technical assistance for peregrine falcons to be captive-raised for eventual release to a new home in Rochester. They coordinated the project, gathering the necessary equipment, money, volunteers, and ideas. Thanks to the company and its fund-raising efforts, the project budget of thirty thousand dollars was met entirely by corporate and individual donations. No tax or conservation funds were required from the state of New York. A total of twelve captive-bred peregrine falcons were released in the Rochester area as a result of the project.

To try to prevent outbreaks of disease, breeding program staff must take several precautions. Initially, the birds must be removed directly from the wild or from facilities where only birds of their species have been cared for so they will not carry diseases from one species of bird to another or spread diseases to other species. Also, breeding facility staff must not care for any other animals, because they could carry diseases from these animals to the endangered raptor. Most importantly, breeding facilities must be closed to the public so that the birds will not inadvertently be exposed to any diseases that humans might carry. Noel Snyder, member of the Condor Recovery Team said, "Unless such efforts are made, the risks of introducing exotic [nonnative] pathogens into captive and wild populations are substantial."[28]

Breeding and raising captive raptors

Another step to complete before housing captive raptors is to create an environment in which each species of captive raptors will feel comfortable breeding. Breeding raptor pairs must not see or have any contact with humans, since such a disturbance in the wild easily disrupts breeding behavior and can cause a pair to abandon a nest site.

In the case of the California condors, scientists designed nesting pens nicknamed "condormitoriums" with screened areas or blinds through which they could observe the birds without the birds seeing them. The birds were placed side by side in adjoining pens to allow the extremely social condors to feel as if they were still in a flock. Inside the pen were ponds for bathing and drinking, large branches and sticks the condors could use for roosts, and cave-like nest boxes that resembled nesting sites they would use in the wild. One roosting perch in the pens was also a scale, which allowed scientists to weigh the birds without having to handle them.

Pairing breeding raptors

Another difficult and important step in the process of captive breeding is pairing the birds that will breed. To give birth to and raise healthy chicks, raptor adults must be caged with another adult they are compatible with both in terms of genetic background and personality. This has proved quite a challenge for some captive-breeding program staff. The Peregrine Fund's early efforts to breed peregrine falcons in captivity did not work because some of the first ones taken from nests in Alaska did not get along with each other and failed to breed. The Fund's scientists had to swap members of pairs until the birds found suitable mates.

In some cases, just making certain that a pair are male and female can be difficult. Before the Condor Recovery Team could begin breeding the California condor, a researcher with experience raising Andean condors conducted DNA testing of each bird's blood cells to determine whether it was male or female, since male and female condors look exactly alike. Next, the team paired individuals that were not closely related to ensure they would produce viable, healthy chicks.

Genetic problems

Such attention to the genetic background of raptors is essential to the success of a captive-breeding program. Genetic problems can present many challenges to producing a releasable population. For example, inbreeding can cause captive raptors to become more susceptible to diseases formerly unknown to their species. Nature writer Roger Pasquier described such a problem with the Mauritius kestrels, "It is likely that inbreeding and a reduced immunity to alien pathogens, a characteristic of island faunas, had increased the birds' vulnerability to disease."[29]

Some researchers also fear that species raised in captivity become too tame to release in the wild. Those birds with genes for tame behavior adapt more easily to captivity and so are more likely to mate and pass on these genes. Noel Snyder, a founding member of the Condor Recovery Team, says that "upon release such captive stocks may be incapable of producing viable wild populations and/or may exert . . . genetic pressures on remnant wild populations."[30]

To reduce the danger that genes for tameness may be bred into a captive population, biologists must return raptors to the wild within a few generations, whether or not necessary habitat has been set aside or the dangers that caused the bird's decline have been removed.

Incubating raptor eggs

Even when breeding is successful and the eggs removed from the captive pairs appear fertile, incubation conditions must closely duplicate those found in the wild nests of that species of raptor. Without the proper temperature and humidity for incubating the eggs, they will die. Such was the case with the Peregrine Fund's early attempts to incubate eggs: They used the same incubation conditions used for hatching chickens. The eggs became too hot and the embryos died. Only after making careful adjustments to heat and humidity within the incubation chambers were Peregrine Fund scientists able to hatch captive-bred peregrine chicks.

The raptor incubation process must carefully duplicate the natural conditions of the bird's own habitat.

Double clutching

Once a pair of captive birds begins to produce eggs, scientists can take advantage of their tendency to "double clutch." Just as birds in the wild lay extra eggs to replace ones that have been removed from a nest, so captive birds will replace eggs that have been removed for artificial incubation. Peregrine Fund scientists removed the first two clutches of eggs from each captive-raised peregrine pair so that the birds would lay a third clutch. The technique of double clutching allows scientists to restore a wild population faster than they could have by allowing captive birds to lay only one clutch per breeding season. After two weeks of being cared for by Peregrine Fund scientists in an incubation chamber, clutches of peregrine falcon chicks were returned to the nests of captive peregrines for rearing.

Double clutching was also used effectively with California condors. Scientists with the Condor Recovery Team removed eggs from captive California condor parents so that each pair would lay another egg. Because California condors raise only one chick every other year, double clutching helps replenish the wild population more quickly than natural breeding would allow.

Learning to be a bird

Ideally, young captive birds of prey targeted for reintroduction to the wild are raised by their own parents or by other captive adults of their own species so that they learn

Because birds lay eggs to replace missing ones, scientists sometimes collect and incubate the first eggs to get a bird to lay more eggs.

behaviors necessary for survival, just as they would in the wild. Allowing adult raptors to raise the young carries some risk for the chicks, but that risk, many believe, is justified. *Smithsonian* writer Jeff Wheelright explains the benefits of allowing a wild raptor to raise young: "Ironically, there's more risk of injury to chicks from 'parent'-rearing, but the contact may make the young birds better parents themselves when they breed in the wild and has the added benefit of reducing their links with humans."[31] Many of the California condors released in the condor recovery program were indeed raised by wild, condor parents.

Imprinting

Young birds learn by imitating their caretakers. This is called "imprinting." If these caretakers are adult birds of their species, the young learn or imprint appropriate survival skills and are likely to breed successfully. If the caretakers are humans, however, the birds may not learn enough survival skills and may not be able to breed. In the case of the Mauritius kestrel, one of the few captive-raised females had become attached to humans as companions and refused to mate with a male kestrel, interpreting his mating behavior as aggression from an unfamiliar species. Similarly, those Philippine eagles that came to a reintroduction program as youngsters illegally removed from the wild had so imprinted on humans that they were hostile with potential mates and, in some cases, even killed them.

Imprinting on humans can cause a wide range of problems. Birds of prey "need to learn such essential skills as how and where to forage and how to respond to potential threats such as predators, competitors, and humans"[32] from others of their species. Human-imprinted raptors do not learn these behaviors and cannot be released to the wild.

Researchers in raptor reintroduction programs have had to greatly modify handling techniques to prevent imprinting. Only by feeding and handling raptor chicks with minimal human contact can recovery team members rest assured that the birds will not begin to think of human beings as their own species. For example, in the California

Challenges of Capturing and Housing Raptors

Removing endangered raptors from the wild for captive breeding and reintroduction is not always successful. One unsuccessful example involves the Philippine eagle. In 1996, the Peregrine Fund obtained a permit from the Philippine government to remove four young Philippine eagles from the wild solely for the purpose of captive breeding. However, one eagle died at the breeding facilities, and though evidence showed that the eagle suffered from malnourishment prior to its removal from the nest, the government suspended the permit for removal of additional birds.

This setback compounded earlier difficulties with finding individual Philippine eagles suitable for captive breeding. In the 1980s, eagles originally planned for captive breeding became available because they had injuries that made them unreleasable or because they had been illegally removed from the wild as youngsters. None of these individuals, as it turned out, were good candidates for captive breeding. The injuries to the first group of birds, made them unable to mate, and the second group could not breed with their own kind because they had imprinted, or bonded as companions, with their human handlers.

To date, the captive-breeding program has had only limited success. In 1992, two captive-bred eagles were hatched. During the 1996 breeding season, four females laid six eggs, but none was fertile. Despite early failure, conservationists still hold out hope for the successful birth of more captive-bred Philippine eagles.

Condor Recovery Program, condors were touched and fed only by puppets made to look like adult condors, operated by human handlers from behind a curtain.

Biologists in captive-breeding programs must ensure that those raptors not raised by raptor parents have adequate time to socialize with others of their species before they are reintroduced to the wild. If a reintroduced bird cannot relate properly to others of its kind, it is unlikely to breed and contribute to the species' recovery. With this goal in mind, four-month-old California condor chicks were moved from the indoor facilities to outdoor pens with other condors to begin the socialization process of learning instinctive hunting and defense behaviors essential to their survival in the wild.

Releasing birds into the wild

When captive-raised birds are moved from captive-breeding facilities in preparation for release, they must be kept at what wild life rehabilitators call "hack-out sites" where they are cared for and observed with minimal human contact. The young raptors are first contained in boxes where they become comfortable with being outdoors. Gradually, when the raptor is ready to fly, its box is opened, allowing it to leave. For a limited time, the young bird can then return to the hack-out site for food. Always, the effort is made to mimic conditions faced by wild raptors. In the case of the peregrine falcon, the hack box is sealed after about six weeks and no more food is provided, since six weeks is about the time after which a falcon would no longer depend on its parents for food.

Often, young raptors need time to adjust to a site before actually being released into it. After several weeks in the hack-out box, some raptors are released into a connecting flight pen where they can make practice flights and become accustomed to the release site's natural surrounding and to weather conditions. For a California condor population released into the bird's former range in Arizona, the lengthy hack-out enclosures were constructed approximately seventy five feet from the edge of a cliff that looked out over the canyon where they would be released.

Even when a young bird has adjusted to conditions at a release site, it still may not know how to find food within it. When the hack-out process is complete, reintroduction team members must sometimes continue to provide food at the release sight until the raptors can hunt on their own. These feeding sites are moved progressively further from the release site so the raptors begin to leave the area to search for their own food. By traveling far from the release site in search of food placed there by the recovery team, the birds are likely to come across similar food in the wild. Team members track the birds; once they see the birds feeding on their own, they cut back on the supplemental food.

Transition to the Wild

Though the gradual hacking-out process for a raptor may sound relatively simple, it depends entirely upon the cooperation of each bird. Those in charge of the harpy eagle reintroduction in Panama wrote on their Peregrine Fund web site that they worried the male and female released from the hack-out site would fly too far from the supplemental food placed at the sight by volunteers to ever find it again: "Our biggest concern is that the eagles will become frightened and fly away before they have learned to return to the release site to feed. If that were to occur before they are ready, it might be extremely difficult to find them." Just as the reintroduction team had feared, the eagles did fly farther into the forest canopy than they had hoped and had difficulty penetrating the trees to reach the food. However, team members were able to feed the birds by pulling food up to them by a rope without revealing to the birds that they were being fed by humans.

Keeping track

Once released, birds of prey must be monitored by a reintroduction team's staff. Prior to release, wing tags or leg bands with identification numbers are attached to each bird to facilitate tracking the bird's movements. In the early days following a release, volunteers often stay at a sight to watch the birds. Some released raptors are fitted with a radio transmitter, satellite telemetry, or other tracking device.

Reintroduced raptors must be monitored for a number of reasons. Some obvious purposes for tracking them are to ensure that they are healthy, out of danger, and have not moved into areas where they cannot be protected. Scientists also monitor reintroduced raptors to see if they successfully breed and reproduce. By tracking the bald eagle in New York State in 1996, for example, biologists were able to confirm that of the 198 birds released there, 29 nesting pairs had raised 37 young. Tracking released birds also lets biologists know how much habitat the bird needs to survive. The harpy eagles released in Panama are being tracked by NASA satellites to let scientists know how large their range will be and what dangers they might encounter there.

Keeping reintroduced raptors safe

Even though scientists try to be sure that adequate habitat is available before a raptor is reintroduced to the wild, often hazards remain there that continue to endanger the bird. For example, cities provide a large habitat free from the DDT that nearly wiped out the peregrine falcon, but they also present other newer hazards that cannot be addressed. For example, the birds must navigate around many obstacles such as aircraft, buildings, and other structures. Also, peregrines in urban areas must contend with maintenance and construction workers who may unintentionally disturb nests.

Outside urban areas, newly released birds face other dangers. For example, Condor Recovery Team workers in Arizona had to solve the problem of electric power poles. Workers knew that condors would be electrocuted because their size caused them to come in contact with two wires at a time. To solve this problem, the team installed mock electric poles in the pre-release pen which gave the birds a mild shock when they landed on them. The birds quickly learned that trees provided a safer perch.

A peregrine chick raised in captivity encourages those who run other breeding projects.

Since harassment by humans is often the greatest danger raptors face, recovery workers try to instill a healthy fear of humans in the birds. Condor Recovery Team members who had to take blood samples or attach wing ID tags to the birds ran at them and handled them roughly. This helped the condors develop a natural aversion to humans. One biologist in the program explained the seemingly cruel treatment: "These harassments, as we sometimes call them—they make some biologists uncomfortable. But we hope to see model condor citizens out there."[33] Ironic as it may seem, even though humans may be an endangered raptor's best friend, they can also be its worst enemy.

Hostility from human neighbors

When they are ready to reintroduce a threatened raptor to its former range, many reintroduction program members face indifference, misunderstanding, and even hostility from people living in or near the release area. Often the mere presence of a protected bird of prey can be seen as an obstacle to local people's way of life. In the 1970s, for example, local foresters in the Philippines feared reintroduction and protection of the Philippine eagle because they saw it as a direct threat to their ability to continue to log the country's forests. Loggers reasoned that they would only be free to harvest timber when there were no longer any eagles in the forests.

Condors faced similar opposition. When a second population of California condors was to be reintroduced thirty miles north of Grand Canyon National Park, many residents of Utah, where the birds were expected to range, feared the bird's presence would mean only trouble for them. Jeff Wheelright describes the problem: "Fundamentally, the Utahans were concerned that the far-ranging condors, alighting on private ranches or public grazing range, might interfere with their use of the land."[34] Some residents feared being fined or put in jail if they accidentally killed or injured a California condor, since harming an endangered species is a federal crime.

The U.S. Fish and Wildlife Service met concerned Utah residents halfway by guaranteeing that a number of protective measures would be put into effect. They agreed to remove birds from private property if the locals found their livelihoods affected. Also, residents were reassured that fines and penalties would only be imposed if someone intentionally killed a bird. Most importantly, the Fish and Wildlife Service promised that the Arizona population of the bird would be listed as a threatened but nonessential experimental population rather than as an endangered one. While this threatened classification still protected the birds from human attack, it allowed for management measures that would not restrict human activity in the region. Residents agreed to the proposal.

Delisting Controversy

Nature writer Les Line and other biologists and conservationists like him criticize the proposed delisting of the peregrine falcon as a purely political maneuver. They say that high peregrine release and overall population numbers are being used to convince critics of the Endangered Species Act that the legislation is indeed working to save animals. Line says in a *National Wildlife* article,

> politics rather than biology is driving the delisting process. Robert Mesta, the Fish and Wildlife Service scientist in charge of monitoring the peregrine's population and seeing that it meets Endangered Species Act goals, says that the high numbers truly represent success: "The people who complain that we shouldn't delist the peregrine should step back and look at the big picture. . . . [The Fish and Wildlife Service] wants to demonstrate that the Endangered Species Act is working, and the peregrine falcon is the perfect, high-profile candidate."

Breeding false optimism

Captive breeding and reintroduction can help pull a species back from the brink of extinction. But the very success of the program can pose a danger. Occasionally, successful captive-breeding and reintroduction programs have led to a misunderstanding of the health of a species. For example, high peregrine falcon numbers have led U.S. Fish and Wildlife Service and other government officials to suggest removing the bird from the endangered species list. Despite these high numbers of peregrine falcons, biologists familiar with the bird and its existing habitat are concerned that the statistics do not accurately portray the species' situation. Many peregrines were reintroduced to urban environments, which is quite different from a healthy population living in the wild, natural environment. In the east, for example, peregrines have not returned to most of their former habitat such as the Appalachian Mountain range.

Many people studying the peregrine say the high urban populations' numbers threaten to overshadow the real problems facing wild populations in the rest of the United

States. Biologist Les Line says, "Simply put, there is concern that the falcon still is affected seriously by pesticides in some parts of the country and that critical goals in the recovery plan for the species have not been met."[35]

Beyond captive breeding and reintroduction

After several decades of breeding raptors in captivity, program organizers have recognized a problem that was not as obvious in the early years: breeding raptors in captivity leads to a false sense that the species are safe and that the need for habitat protection is not as urgent. Even Noel Snyder, an integral member of the Condor Recovery Team, said that, despite success with breeding condors in captivity, the California condor's habitat still contains hazards that have not been addressed. He says that

> despite requests over a period of years from the California Condor Recovery Team, the U.S. Fish and Wildlife Service has until recently declined to fund a proposal to conduct toxicity studies of alternatives to lead bullets, which could solve the problem of lead poisoning in Condors in the wild. Meanwhile captive breeding and releases have continued to be funded at more than $1.0 million annually.[36]

Despite the controversies surrounding captive breeding and reintroduction, many conservationists believe that after thirty years of experience with the technique, it represents one of the best means of preventing extinction of a bird of prey. Around the world, governments and individuals are making efforts to secure safe habitats and migration corridors for both reintroduced endangered birds of prey and those remaining in the wild.

Captive breeding and reintroduction is just one sign that the desire to protect endangered birds of prey is growing. Migratory raptor counts, public education efforts, and habitat preservation also have made some conservationists feel hopeful about the future and have increased the chances of survival for many birds of prey.

5

Worldwide Recovery Efforts

THOUGH MANY REFUGES and wilderness areas around the world contain habitat for endangered birds of prey, no one knows for sure whether these areas will withstand the pressure of increasing human demand for land and resources. Given the current human population growth, conservationists have valid reason for concern.

However, some people who once felt that many species of raptor had no hope of survival feel a flicker of optimism. Ecotourism and environmental education programs have begun to influence the lifestyles and thinking of people living near endangered birds of prey. Because of such programs, some people have begun to appreciate and understand the logic behind preserving a threatened raptor as part of a larger ecosystem.

Also, corporations have been increasingly willing to discuss with governments and conservation groups the ways they might work together to save endangered raptors. Though disagreements between environmentalists and corporations still exist, some attempts have been made to remove resources from raptor habitat while still preserving existing populations.

Though pressure to develop land along raptor migration corridors still exists, countries around the world are newly aware of the effect humans have on migrating raptors. Migratory bird counts have become an important way of tracking the health of threatened species and a

Ranchers Can Coexist with Raptors

With patience and education, even those who once thought otherwise can come to see the truth about a bird of prey rather than continue to believe the myths that the birds have evil natures and mean people harm. Bruce Beans, author of *Eagle's Plume,* describes how one rancher now coexists with bald eagles: "Twenty-five years ago Carey Lightsey, a sixth generation cattle rancher in central Florida, rarely saw a bald eagle. On his ranch now are fourteen nests. He says, 'People ask me, "My God there are eagles everywhere. How do you even operate?" But it's never affected us. If there's one thing I learned being raised on a ranch, it's that we can live with eagles.'"

way to educate people about the special struggles the birds face on their journey.

Promise of environmental education

Through an environmental education program, people living near endangered raptor populations can be made aware of the beneficial roles raptors play in maintaining balance in the environment. In some cases, people have come to view raptors as allies instead of enemies. For example, farmers in Argentina are beginning to understand how useful Swainson's hawks can be in naturally controlling the grasshopper populations that have devastated their crops. Often, the easiest way to convince local people of the beneficial role raptors play is to explain to them that raptors feed on nuisance animals.

Environmental educators who share the same home and nationality as their audience have been especially effective at convincing people to protect an endangered raptor. Rather than being seen as outsiders, these native educators can address the needs of endangered species in ways people of their homeland are more likely to accept. For example, harpy eagle protection in Venezuela has become easier as native Venezuelan and Peregrine Fund biologist Eduardo Alvarez has educated local children and adults about the value of the bird. Writer Les Line reports that even "loggers in a chain-saw crew recently stopped cutting when they looked up and spotted an eagle on its nest. They said, 'Let's call Eduardo.' The loggers adopted and protected the nest site and now there's a full-grown chick."[37]

Mutual respect

By making sure that their educational program reflected an understanding of the nation's economy as well as teaching the people about the Philippine eagle, the Philippine Eagle Foundation, Inc. gained the attention and assistance of many Filipinos. After educating people about the bird and its habits, the foundation offered a "nest reward" program that paid the finder money for locating nests with healthy eagles in it. Environmental educators also worked with local residents to develop alternative agricultural methods to the slash-and-burn farming (cutting trees and burning the land for agriculture) that had been destroying the habitat the Philippine eagle needs to survive. By 1996, four hundred families had benefited from the programs started by the Philippine Eagle Foundation.

Another foundation educational program, "Classrooms That Make a Difference," taught Filipino elementary and secondary school students about the importance of reforestation, a crucial task if the Philippine eagle is to survive at all, considering its quickly dwindling habitat. With the help of the foundation and the local Parent Teacher Community Association, students replanted a patch of rain forest habitat. If the Philippine eagle can sustain its current population numbers, it will need this replanted forest for future habitat.

Understanding is the key

Before beginning to educate a community about an endangered raptor population in their area, an environmental educator must understand the needs and concerns of people in the community. Only by talking with and getting to

A park ranger counts migrating birds in Cardel, Mexico.

know the local people can environmentalists know what dangers the bird actually faces and what local concerns must be addressed. For example, if indiscriminate hunting endangers the raptor, then the most important and probably most difficult audience member to reach will be the hunter. Ernesto Inzunza, director of the environmental organization Pronatura faces just such a difficult audience in his attempts to protect many raptors such as Swainson's hawks, Mississippi kites, and kestrels that seasonally migrate through the area near Veracruz, Mexico. Because farmers continue to clear forest to plant crops such as corn, the raptors are forced to roost in the open, on the few trees that remain, where they are vulnerable to poachers and people who trap the birds illegally. Inzunza notes that though the farmers acknowledge the problems the raptors face, they still do not understand the role they play in creating these problems:

> The farmers are very curious and very open. . . . They know where the roost sites are and who's shooting or trapping birds illegally. But they are still cutting the sides of the hills to plant corn . . . because they've burned the rest of the land, and it has lost most of its nutrients. They can use it only four or five years. . . . Some of us work with the farmers with what they do with the habitat. We're also trying to stop the direct persecution of the birds. . . . We need to educate [the farmers] . . . [38]

Raising awareness

Another challenge to education programs is raising local awareness about a raptor or a migration of raptors that is very familiar to the local people and that they may not see as valuable. When asked, for example, if the people of Veracruz, Mexico, appreciated the enormous raptor migration through their area each season, Pronatura director Ernesto Inzunza said, "They've always been aware of the hawks, but, no, the people don't know how special they are, and that is also part of our education objectives."[39] Through its education program, Pronatura is now working to make the local people aware of just how unusual such a migration of raptors actually is—that though it may seem commonplace to them, such a phenomenon is known in only a few other places on earth.

Redesigning educational materials

Environmental educators must also tailor presentations to the varied language and education levels of the audience. For example, a staff member of Pronatura, Sandra L. Mesa Ortiz, had to take into account that many of the people she was trying to reach were not able to read. Ortiz has completely redesigned her educational materials to reach the local Veracruz children in particular, since the hope for future conservation efforts rests primarily in their hands. What came out of this effort, according to writer Jessica Maxwell,

> is a brilliant set of hands-on activities now enjoyed by six Veracruz elementary schools and 300 students each year. There is the pesticide skit, in which students play roles from the hawk and the grasshopper to the farmer and the shopper. "The point is that pesticides travel," Sandra explained. "They get to your table. The hawk gets sick, and what happens to the hawk is happening to you."[40]

Environmental education has helped reduce the killing of endangered birds worldwide.

Teaching local teachers

As environmental educators look to the future, they realize that the most important group of people to speak to are the children, but sometimes the local school teachers need instruction about the environment as well. If an educational program is to have any long-term effectiveness, local teachers must become an integral part of it. For example, the Pronatura staff in Veracruz, Mexico, has made a special effort to instruct local schoolteachers about basic environmental concepts so that they, in turn, could teach elementary school children about the raptors migrating through the area.

Money and time

Not surprisingly, environmental education programs require a large amount of money and time if they are to be effective. In many cases, the people who need to be reached are spread out over a large area of rugged terrain, making travel for environmental workers expensive and hazardous. To conduct environmental education programs, organizations must constantly apply for grants from governments, environmental groups, corporations, and individuals.

Moreover, environmental education is not a quick fix. It often requires years of persistence. Ultimately, an environmental education program is only as successful as people's understanding and acceptance of what they learn. An organization's long-term presence in an area and repeated efforts to educate the people may be necessary before it produces any results.

Habitat conservation plans

Besides educational outreach, those who want to save endangered birds of prey often find they must work with corporations whose activities pose a threat to the birds. In larger countries, many corporations now want to lessen the impact they have on birds of prey by funding and designing conservation programs that will allow them to conduct business and protect the birds at the same time. Proponents of such programs say that if endangered raptors are to survive, they must do so in environments they share with humans.

Recently, the U.S. government and some corporations have worked together to develop a way to make use of natural resources as well as protect endangered birds of prey and other animals. The result of this collaboration is known as a habitat conservation plan (HCP). Under an HCP, federal, state, or local governments can combine payments from landholders and their own conservation funding to purchase crucial habitat for endangered birds of prey and then change zoning laws to protect the area from any future development.

For example, as a compromise in the northern spotted owl debate, Weyerhaeuser, a wood products company, and the U.S. Fish and Wildlife Service drew up an HCP designed to allow logging activities and the northern spotted owl to coexist. According to the HCP, Weyerhaeuser will provide what is called "dispersal habitat" on land it owns. This habitat will provide the northern spotted owl with tracts of land for hunting and nesting or for moving between federal and state protected sections of habitat. The HCP also says that the Weyerhaeuser Company will provide protection from human interference on its land. In effect for fifty years, the HCP also says that Weyerhaeuser

Compromises between industry and government allow the use of natural resources as well as the protection of endangered birds of prey.

must use careful tree-harvesting practices so that the owl's habitat on their land will not be destroyed.

Where the Endangered Species Act once fostered an uncooperative attitude among U.S. developers and private corporations, HCPs have changed some people's attitudes. For example, a recent version of an HCP called "Safe Harbor" has worked toward protecting the aplomado falcon, the most endangered of all North American falcons. The bird once lived in the tall, natural grasslands of Texas and New Mexico, but practices such as overgrazing changed the height, quantity, and health of the grasses, making them no longer suitable as a breeding area for the falcon. *Audubon* writer Ted Williams reports that "now, in exchange for a promise from the Fish and Wildlife Service to let them develop their land as they see fit, ranchers have given the Peregrine Fund permission to construct towers on which young falcons are raised and released to the wild. A million acres have been enrolled, and the fund is now releasing about one hundred birds a year. Wild nesting resumed in 1995."[41] The Fish and Wildlife Service hopes that such enthusiasm from corporations and landholders continues.

Ranchers have allowed towers to be constructed on their land to safely raise aplomado falcon chicks in exchange for a guarantee that they may develop their land without government interference.

Suspicions about HCPs

Not everyone agrees that HCPs are a good solution to the problem of habitat destruction. Ted Williams describes the controversial changes to the Endangered Species Act that have allowed for HCPs:

> Amendments . . . allow the Fish and Wildlife Service to offer an incentive for endangered-species conservation. Curiously enough, they permit a landowner to destroy the very habitat on which a listed species depends. In exchange for such a permit, the landowner must "mitigate" the loss by any means federal biologists deem best for that species. For example, a permit to put up condominiums might obligate the landowner to provide money with which the Fish and Wildlife Service or another entity can buy similar habitat elsewhere . . .[42]

A clear-cut hillside starkly contrasts with the dense habitat of the northern spotted owl.

To some people on both sides of the debate over endangered species, HCPs do not represent the solution. Environmentalists are still suspicious of HCPs, believing they weaken the Endangered Species Act and further threaten endangered species. Critics of HCPs believe, in fact, that HCPs simply represent a license to conduct business as usual.

Criticism of HCPs has arisen out of the northern spotted owl controversy. Those who oppose the Weyerhaeuser HCP question even its basic premise, the "dispersal habitat." The problem, they say, lies in the fact that dispersal habitats consist of second-growth forest instead of old-growth forest. Old-growth forests are made up of ancient trees as opposed to second-growth which means a region of younger replanted trees. Northern spotted owls, say these environmentalists, will fly through the dispersal habitat of unsuitable second-growth stands in search of the small already overpopulated remaining old-growth stands. Second-growth stands do not provide necessary habitat for the prey species that northern spotted owls depend upon to survive. Biologists who have studied the northern spotted owl predict they will not adapt to second-growth forest habitat set aside for them.

Landholders and developers have their own problems with HCPs, though for different reasons than environmentalists. Many still view the Endangered Species Act and its defenders as the enemy and will not cooperate with the Fish and Wildlife Service in implementing HCPs on their property. As writer Ted Williams says, "old impressions die hard, and developers and property-rights types still tend to think of the Endangered Species Act [and the HCPs it gave birth to] as a bogeyman."[43] They would rather do without what they perceive as interference with their operations and decision making.

Despite the controversies arising from agreements like the HCPs, for corporations to adapt their business plans to accommodate an endangered raptor represents a change in the way people view their place in the environment. No longer is the death or displacement of a creature of little concern. Around the world, corporations are beginning to take seriously the impact they have on raptor habitat. Even as some companies have discovered that profits and respect for endangered habitat are compatible, others have discovered that there is money to be earned by sharing the beauty and fascination that wild animals and birds offer through a form of outreach known as ecotourism.

The destruction of northern spotted owl habitat brought the HCP controversy into the national spotlight.

Ecotourism signals interest in raptors

Ecotourism means that instead of paying money to attend recreational events or amusement parks, for example, tourists pay to see a part of the local ecosystem of their destination. Ecotourism provides opportunities for people to appreciate and protect endangered birds of prey. Raptor migration watch sites and observation areas have sprung up around the world, allowing tourists to see the birds in their environment. One of the hopes for ecotourism is that the people who see and learn about raptors will go on to do things to ensure their survival.

Ecotourism can also benefit an endangered bird of prey by benefiting the local people who have the most control over its survival. Ecotourism provides economic reasons for the inhabitants of an area to protect an endangered raptor whose habitat they may have been using in ways that would not sustain it. Often the residents of an area can be educated about the bird and the place it lives so that they can make money by participating in ecotours themselves. This also gives them a newfound appreciation for the raptor.

Also, ecotourism often injects much-needed money into a struggling local economy. Ecotourism can provide ways for local people to make money that protects rather than further endangers an endangered raptor. In Cardel, Mexico, the main hawk migration counting city, the station is located atop a local inn called the Hotel Bienvenidos. The owner of the building has benefited so much from the ecotourism dollars spent by people coming to view the migration that he changed his logo to include a Mississippi kite, one of the birds that passes through the area.

The most successful ecotourism ventures similarly involve local residents as much as possible. If residents are involved in the planning stages of an effort, they feel a sense of ownership in the venture. Also, tour operators who make use of the local labor force to provide services such as transportation, food, lodging, and even guides and interpreters, can quickly receive the support of residents formerly suspicious of those who appear to value raptors over people. One ecotour operator who made a point to hire only

Mississippi kites pass through Cardel, Mexico, a popular site to watch migrating birds.

natives to staff his tours said, "We firmly believe that legitimate conservation efforts must integrate the local people."[44]

Ecotourism bolsters economies

A Peruvian ecotour focusing on the endangered harpy eagle demonstrates the power of a carefully planned and managed ecotourism effort that involves local residents, the Ese'eja Indians living in the village of Infierno. For some time, the Ese'eja made their livings as subsistence farmers and hunters and by selling plant products they collected from the forests and processed themselves.

With modernization has come problems for the Ese'eja, as Tui De Roy, a writer for *International Wildlife* explains: "Better standards of living also brought the loss of traditional values and, with this, a sense of aimlessness. . . . And with guns replacing the bows and arrows of old, the over-harvesting of jungle species became a pressing issue."[45] One of these jungle species was the harpy eagle, which the natives killed for food. They also hunted the harpy's prey, leaving very little for the birds to survive on.

Eduardo Nycander, an architect and native of Lima, Peru, began a program in the area both to raise money for research into studying and saving the eagles and to help the Ese'eja people create an economy supplemented largely by ecotourism. Nycander formed an ecotourism company, Rainforest Expeditions, that raises money for research into the health of the harpy eagle and employs native Ese'eja Indians as guides, boat drivers, and support staff. The Ese'eja also helped build lodges and tour facilities and participated in job-training workshops to prepare for the several dozen high-paying tourists who visit the site annually for a peek at the magnificent harpy eagle.

As money from ecotourism bolstered the economy of their community, the Ese'eja joined forces with Nycander to form the Ke'eway Association (Ke'eway is the Ese'eja name for harpy eagle). As part of a twenty-year contract, they divide the profits of ecotourism. Understanding the economic benefit to protecting the harpy eagle, the Ke'eway Association has set aside fifteen hundred acres of wilderness habitat for the bird and has passed local laws to protect them from being shot or their nest areas from being disturbed.

Ecotourism in the United States

Though it is a nation whose residents are thought to be among the most environmentally aware in the world, the United States has its own share of ecotourism activity with a goal of helping people appreciate birds of prey they may not have understood or even been aware of before. Though the financial issues are not the same in a large nation with more resources and abundant land to set aside as refuges, tours still must be conducted in a way that respects the area and all of its residents.

For example, Hawk Mountain, a raptor watch site in Kempton, Pennsylvania, protects threatened birds of prey such as the bald eagle and greatly benefits its surrounding community, where ecotourists "annually support approximately 150 restaurants, 43 hotels, motels, and guest houses, and 23 campsites."[46] Many of these establishments have included Hawk Mountain in their names.

A Utah-based conservation organization called Hawk-watch preserved 485,000 acres of relatively untouched land near the Snake River in Idaho, where, under the careful supervision of guides, tourists can view the densest concentration of nesting raptors in North America. On bus and boat tours of this federally protected area, people have the chance to witness the natural behavior of some eight hundred resident breeding pairs of raptors. Species include golden eagles, red-tailed hawks, Swainson's hawks, northern harriers, American kestrels, and at least six species of owls. Many of the species living there are threatened, but on the land maintained by Hawkwatch, raptors can breed and rear their young without being disturbed by humans.

Limitations of ecotourism

Properly conducted, ecotours benefit birds of prey and local human populations. Even though ecotourism can do many good things for birds of prey, if run by tour organizers who leave local residents out of the planning stages, a tour can create even more bad feelings about a bird of prey. Tour operators sometimes make the mistake of ignoring

An influx of tourists can pose problems for local bird populations.

the local labor force available to staff their tours and come to be seen as invaders who unfairly use resources.

Tourism can damage site

Tour operators often find that ecotourism is a balancing act. Operators must do all they can to preserve the uniqueness of a local culture, even those who use local residents to staff their tours. K. L. Bildstein and J. I. Zalles describe one danger that ecotourism represents for indigenous people: "It is essential that the cultural identity of local populations remain intact as far as possible during the course of [ecotourist] activities. Human populations in [undeveloped] locations are especially vulnerable to being swamped by economic opportunities associated with tourism."[47]

Even properly run ecotours are not a complete solution to the problem of protecting endangered raptors. Since the influx of tourists is neither steady nor reliable, the income ecotourism generates must be seen as a supplement to money coming from private foundations and government grants.

North-South American migration

All the efforts at habitat preservation, protective legislation, and outreach to local people and tourists cannot save a bird that migrates from a safe location to one where it is unprotected. Raptor migration poses unique challenges as well as opportunities.

In the spring and fall, many birds of prey travel over what biologists call a bottleneck, or a kind of funnel of lowland in Central America on their way to and from their summer and winter homes. As the birds pass through the area, biologists and other observers have the chance to make accurate estimates of migratory raptor populations. Migration counts provide some of the best information about the health of endangered migratory raptor species because most of the population will fly seasonally through a predictable area. Many times these counts serve as an early warning of problems ahead such as the effects of overhunting, forestry, or pesticide use.

International migration agreement

As the birds migrate, of course, they pass through the jurisdiction of various nations. The amount of protection these raptors receive can vary widely. For example, though in the United States the pesticide monocrotophos has been banned, in South America it is still used to control grasshoppers that Swainson's hawks eat and are consequently poisoned by. Protecting birds of prey who travel from one country to another and one level of legal protection to another is not an entirely new concept. The Migratory Bird Treaty Act was enacted in 1918 to encourage internationally consistent protection for migrating raptors and other birds by protecting them from hunting and other human interference. However, the treaty's authors could not have anticipated the vast habitat destruction now present on virtually every continent.

In 1980, Senator George Mitchell of Maine sponsored an amendment to the treaty to regulate human activities and the resulting habitat loss that affected bird populations. Just as important, the U.S. National Fish and Wildlife Federation gathered 150 scientists, teachers, and politicians to form Partners in Flight, an international organization to promote compliance with the Mitchell Amendment. Partners in Flight proposes to help in various ways. Among other things, Partners in Flight funds educational efforts at the elementary, secondary, and university levels on the importance of preserving habitats and protecting birds of prey. Other efforts include coordinating the financial and technical participation of corporations in researching, managing and monitoring populations of endangered raptors, and in setting aside migration resting sites. Yet even with the protections afforded by the Mitchell Amendment, migratory raptors still face problems.

Researchers gather at a raptor counting site in Chichicaxtle, Mexico, one of many international efforts to protect migrating birds.

Migration Watch in Israel
In the town of Elat, Israel, bird watchers can witness another seasonal raptor migration as the birds make their way from northern Africa and southern Europe to northern Europe, Russia, and Asia. Reuven Yosef, Director of the International Birding Center headquartered in Elat, says that as many as six hundred thousand raptors travel across the area each spring and fall. These raptors ride thermals unique to this area of the Middle East.

The bird sanctuary at Elat, which was converted from a sanitary landfill, provides a much-needed feeding and resting place for the migrating raptors, which have a difficult, exhausting journey ahead. They must cross twenty-five hundred miles of some of the harshest desert terrain in the world to migrate back and forth from their seasonal mating grounds in Russia and Asia.

Weakness of migratory agreements

The difficulty with international migratory agreements is that they preside over a vast amount of land and large numbers of people with diverse beliefs and ways of living. Many smaller municipalities, for example, have a hard time reaching the people of their community and enforcing the terms of such agreements. While a bird may be appreciated and rigidly protected in one area, it may be viewed completely differently in another area.

Outlook for the future

Despite the dangers faced by migrating raptors, advocates of birds of prey have many things to be encouraged about. People have taken many steps toward making the planet one in which both humans and birds of prey can live. On the most basic level, more and more people seem aware of these complex and elusive creatures.

In cases like those of the bald eagle, the peregrine falcon, the California condor, and the Mauritius kestrel, combined human efforts to save endangered birds of prey have

Governments Protect Sea Eagle

The sea eagle had become endangered throughout Europe and Scandinavia, until many countries tried to lessen large-scale destruction of its habitat. In Norway and Sweden, the governments set aside prime breeding and nesting habitats. On a small, sparsely populated island off the coast of Finland, the World Wildlife Fund worked with the government to purchase all existing timber in order to protect only two sea eagle eyries. The Finnish government has continued to guard the eyries and has written legislation to protect the sea eagle population. Prior to the reunification of Germany, the East German government made it illegal to cut sea eagle nesting trees and rewarded people with money for every successful brood raised on their property. Poland also preserved key tracts of forest frequented by the bird of prey.

had a positive effect. As naturalist Guy Mountfort writes "projects initiated in despair have occasionally resulted in spectacular successes, proving that if the necessary skill, resources and dedication can be applied endangered species can still be saved."[48] Most important of all to the survival of birds of prey, people now seem to understand that their actions as individuals, however small or isolated they might seem, can affect birds of prey either in positive or negative ways.

Not all of the problems facing birds of prey have been addressed by those concerned with their future. Rapid destruction of habitat and continued pesticide use around the world continue to endanger species. No one can say whether habitat preserved for birds of prey will resist the ever-increasing demand for land and resources. Will these magnificent creatures continue to inspire awe in future generations? That question will be answered by the humans alive today.

Notes

Chapter 1: What Is a Bird of Prey?

1. Philip S. Callahan, *The Magnificent Birds of Prey.* New York: Holiday House, 1974, p. 113.

2. Peter Parnall, *The Daywatchers.* New York: Macmillan, 1984, p. 14.

3. Angus Cameron and Peter Parnall, *The Nightwatchers.* New York: Four Winds Press, 1971, p.11.

Chapter 2: The Problem of Pesticides

4. John Love, *Return of the Sea Eagle.* Cambridge, England: Cambridge University Press, 1983, p. 154.

5. Ted Williams, "Silent Scourge," *Audubon,* January/February, 1997 p. 32.

6. Quoted in Williams, "Silent Scourge," p. 29.

7. Williams, "Silent Scourge," p. 29.

8. Quoted in Frank Graham Jr., "100 Years of Conservation," *Audubon,* November/December 1998, p. 68.

9. *National Parks,* "Falcon Returns to the Smokies," January/February 1998, p. 18.

10. Williams, "Silent Scourge," p. 30.

11. Galen Rowell, "Peregrines in Peril," *Earth Island Journal,* Spring 1997, p. 30.

12. Quoted in Rowell, "Peregrines in Peril," p. 30.

13. Les Line, "Lethal Migration," *Audubon,* September/October 1996, p. 56.

14. Line, "Lethal Migration," p. 95.

15. Quoted in Roger Di Silvestro, "What's Killing the Swainson's Hawk," *International Wildlife,* May/June 1996, p. 41.

16. Line, "Lethal Migration," p. 52.

Chapter 3: The Struggle for Space and Resources

17. James Ferguson-Lees, *Endangered Birds.* London:

George Philip Limited, 1992, p. 14.

18. Bruce Beans, *Eagle's Plume.* New York: Scribners, 1996, p. 218.

19. Quoted in Beans, *Eagle's Plume,* p. 218.

20. Les Line, "Giants of the Eagle Kind," *International Wildlife,* July/August 1996, p. 34.

21. Catherine Lazaroff, "Trouble in the Air," *Audubon,* May/June 1998, p. 117.

22. Rob Edwards, "Bad Sport: Hundreds of Endangered Birds Are Being Killed to Protect a Countryside Pursuit," *New Scientist,* August 9, 1997, p.15.

23. Neil Rettig, "Lords of an Imperiled Realm," *National Geographic,* February 1995, p. 47.

24. Line, "Giants of the Eagle Kind," p. 30.

25. Richard E. Lewis, "A Rain-forest Raptor in Danger," *Oryx,* July 1986, p. 175.

26. Karen Puracan, "The Philippine Eagle: 'King of Birds,'" *Wildlife Rehabilitation Today,* Spring 1996, p. 49.

Chapter 4: Captive Breeding and Reintroduction

27. Kenneth Brower, "The Naked Vulture and the Thinking Ape," *Atlantic Monthly,* October 1983, p. 74.

28. Noel Snyder, "Captive Breeding of Endangered Species," *Conservation Biology,* April 1996, p. 343.

29. Roger Pasquier and Carl Jones, "The Lost and Lonely Birds of Mauritius," *Natural History,* March 1982, p. 41.

30. Snyder, "Captive Breeding," p. 346.

31. Jeff Wheelright, "Condors: Back from the Brink," *Smithsonian,* May 1997, pp. 51–52.

32. Shawn Farry, "California Condors Released at Vermilion Cliffs," February 26, 1998. www.peregrinefund.org/vermil.html.

33. Quoted in Wheelright, "Condors," p. 54.

34. Wheelright, "Condors," p. 50.

35. Les Line, "Symbol of Hope?," *National Wildlife,* October/November 1996, p. 38.

36. Snyder, "Captive Breeding," p. 344.

Chapter 5 : Worldwide Recovery Efforts

37. Line, "Giants of the Eagle Kind," p. 36.

38. Quoted in Jessica Maxwell, "River of Raptors," *Natural History,* October 1996, p. 54.

39. Quoted in Maxwell, "River of Raptors," p. 57.

40. Maxwell, "River of Raptors," p. 52.

41. Ted Williams, "The New Guardians," *Audubon,* January/February 1999, p. 37.

42. Williams, "The New Guardians," p. 36.

43. Williams, "The New Guardians," p. 36.

44. Tui De Roy, "My Treetop Brush with a Harpy," *International Wildlife,* July/August 1998, p. 28.

45. De Roy, "My Treetop Brush with a Harpy," p. 27.

46. K. L. Bildstein and J. I. Zalles, *Hawks Aloft Worldwide: A Cooperative Strategy for Protecting the World's Migratory Raptors–Raptor Migration Watch-site Manual.* Kempton, PA: Hawk Mountain Sanctuary Association, 1995, p. 7.4.

47. Bildstein and Zalles, *Hawks Aloft Worldwide*, p. 7.5.

48. Guy Mountfort, *Rare Birds of the World: A Collins/ICBP Handbook.* Lexington, MA: Stephen Greene Press, 1988, p. 20.

Glossary

---

accipiters: Bird hawks with a typically rapid wing beating flight pattern.

aversion training: To prepare captive raptors for life in the wild, humans may provide them with unpleasant experiences. For example, California condors were given a mild shock from mock electric poles in their pens to help them avoid electrocution in the wild.

bottleneck: In this context, a bottleneck is a narrow strip of land that migrating raptors all fly through on their way to seasonal homes. In other words, they fly close together as if pushed through the narrow neck of a bottle.

buteos: Hawks with broad shoulders, round bodies, and short tails that hunt in wide open landscapes.

captive breeding: The process by which a pair of birds of prey or other animal is removed from the wild so that it can breed within an enclosure without the danger of human interference in the wild.

corridor: An undisturbed strip of land necessary to allow a species to travel from one area of its habitat to another.

delisting: The process by which endangered species are removed from the U.S. Endangered Species List.

dispersal habitat: The land corporations and conservationists have designated as a protected area that raptors affected by development in one part of their habitat can find refuge within. diurnal: Daytime; hawks, eagles, falcons and vultures are diurnal birds of prey.

diurnal: Daytime; hawks, eagles, falcons, and vultures are diurnal birds of prey.

ecotourism: Travel designed to allow the tourist to see a place or animal of environmental interest.

endemic: If a bird of prey or other animal must live in one particular area, an island for example, because of certain habitat characteristics then it is endemic to that area.

eyrie: An eagle's nest.

fratricide: When juvenile birds of prey kill a sibling.

Habitat Conservation Plan (HCP): Recently, corporations have begun to institute Habitat Conservation Plans, or procedures that will allow operations to continue while still protecting an endangered animal.

hack-out: The box or enclosure where birds of prey or other captive wild animals can make the necessary transition back to the wild

imprinting: If a young animal is raised with too much human contact, they begin to "imprint" on humans or view them as parents. Such animals cannot then adapt to life in the wild.

indicator species: When a highly visible species, such as a bird of prey, begins to suffer visibly the effects of an environmental problem that spells danger for other species.

monocrotophos: A pesticide used to protect crops from grasshoppers that indirectly kills the Swainson's hawk, which eats the grasshoppers.

nocturnal: Nighttime; owls are nocturnal birds of prey.

old-growth forest: An ancient forest whose trees haven't been cut or burned for centuries. Many raptors depend on old-growth forest habitat for survival.

organophosphate: Name given to a group of phospherous-containing chemicals widely used as agricultural pesticides.

slash-and-burn farming: In portions of the world's rain forests, people have cut down vegetation and burned the area to prepare it for agricultural crops.

thermals: Seasonal warm currents of air high above the earth's surface that many birds of prey "ride" from one home to another.

Organizations
to Contact

American Bird Conservancy
1250 24th St. NW #500
Washington, DC 20037

A conservation organization dedicated solely to the preservation of birds and their habitat. They work with Latin American countries to reduce pesticide use and preserve raptor habitat.

Hawk Mountain Sanctuary
RR 2, Box 191
Kempton, PA 19529

Called "the place where hawk watching was born," this bird sanctuary monitors seasonal hawk migrations and is a favorite stop for bird watchers. They also provide public education programs.

Hawkwatch International
Salt Lake City, UT 84110-0660

This Utah-based conservation organization has set aside 485,000 acres of land called the Snake River Birds of Prey National Conservation Area in Idaho where the densest concentration of raptors nest in North America.

National Audubon Society
Birds in the Balance Campaign
666 Pennsylvania Ave. SE
Washington, DC 20003

One of the world's first conservation organizations, the National Audubon Society has local chapters throughout the

United States that organize annual bird counts and provide public education programs. On the national level, the organization protects many threatened or endangered animals. Its Birds in the Balance Campaign works specifically to protect endangered birds.

National Wildlife Federation

Laurel Ridge Conservation Education Center
8925 Leesburg Pike
Vienna, VA 22180

The National Wildlife Federation protects wildlife and their habitat and provides public education concerning environmental issues. The organization purchased tracts of Missouri River bottomland to provide wintering sites for the endangered bald eagle. Funded by the National Wildlife Federation, the Laurel Ridge Conservation Education Center provides special public education programs about raptors.

Partners in Flight (Aves de las Americas)

National Fish and Wildlife Foundation
1120 Connecticut Ave. NW, Suite 900
Washington, DC 20036

An organization dedicated to protecting raptors that migrate between North, South, and Central America. A primary goal is to educate students at all age levels about the importance of raptors and other birds.

Peregrine Fund

World Center for Birds of Prey
5666 West Flying Hawk Ln.
Boise, ID 83709

A privately funded organization dedicated to providing the funding and expertise necessary to captive breed and reintroduce endangered birds of prey.

Suggestions for Further Reading

Caroline Arnold, *On the Brink of Extinction: The California Condor.* Orlando, FL: Harcourt Brace Jovanovich, 1993. Excellent description of the delicate process of reintroducing the California condor.

"California Condors in Grand Canyon Area," Peregrine Fund, February 26, 1998. www.peregrinefund.org/vermil.html.

Philip S. Callahan, *The Magnificent Birds of Prey.* New York: Holiday House, 1974. Though primarily intended as a defense of the sport of falconry, this book provides excellent information about nesting and hunting habits of various birds of prey.

Angus Cameron and Peter Parnall, *The Nightwatchers.* New York: Four Winds Press, 1971. Though dated, this book still provides excellent natural histories of North American owls and the author's careful observation of them in the wild.

James Ferguson-Lees, *Endangered Birds.* London: George Philip Limited, 1992. Though less comprehensive than Montefort's *Rare Birds of the World,* this guide provides more recent information about the plight of some rare birds of prey.

Wolfgang Obst and Sharon Obst, *The Condor.* Vestron Video, 1989. This video contains excellent footage of captive breeding and reintroduction of the California condor.

Peter Parnall, *The Daywatchers.* New York: Macmillan, 1984. This book offers good information about individual hawks and provides anecdotes of the author's experiences with these birds in the wild.

"Peregrine Fund Returns Panama's National Bird," Peregrine Fund, February 26, 1998. www.peregrinefund.org/harpypr.html.

"Philippine Eagle Conservation," Peregrine Fund, February 26, 1998. www.peregrinefund.org/philipp.html.

Alvin Silverstein, Virginia Silverstein, and Robert Silverstein, *The Peregrine Falcon.* Brookfield, CT: Millbrook Press, 1995. This book provides an excellent history of the peregrine's recovery in North America.

Alvin Silverstein, Virginia Silverstein, and Robert Silverstein, *The Spotted Owl.* Brookfield, CT: Millbrook Press, 1994. Good background on the issues surrounding the northern spotted owl controversy in the Pacific Northwest but it does not really examine both sides of the issue to any great depth.

Ann Turner, *Vultures.* New York: David McKay Company, 1973. Good introductory book though a bit outdated. It will not, for example, contain any information about the California condor reintroduction.

Works Consulted

Books

Bruce Beans, *Eagle's Plume*. New York: Scribners, 1996. A long, occasionally angry but very useful book about the history of the bald eagle's troubles in North America.

K. L. Bildstein and J. I. Zalles, *Hawks Aloft Worldwide: A Cooperative Strategy for Protecting the World's Migratory Raptors–Raptor Migration Watch-site Manual*. Kempton, PA: Hawk Mountain Sanctuary Association, 1995. A very narrow but useful text for those readers interested in constructing educational programs and migration watch sites that protect migratory raptors. It contains interesting chapters on ecotourism and developing environmental education programs sensitive to the concerns of small countries.

Rachel Carson, *Silent Spring*. Boston: Houghton Mifflin, 1962. The definitive text on pesticides and their dangers. Written in the 1960s, many of this book's predictions have come true.

John Love, *Return of the Sea Eagle*. Cambridge, England: Cambridge University Press, 1983. Though a reader would need to access more recent information about the ultimate success of the sea eagle reintroduction to Great Britain, this is a long but excellent book describing all of the steps to reintroducing a raptor, including the months spent in planning and research.

Guy Mountfort, *Rare Birds of the World: A Collins/ICBP Handbook*. Lexington, MA: Stephen Greene Press, 1988. One of the best comprehensive guides to rare raptors around the world.

Chris Stuart and Tilde Stuart, *Africa's Vanishing Wildlife*. Washington, DC: Smithsonian Institution Press, 1996. Good reference tool to determine species that are endangered and the reasons for each raptor's decline. One of the more recent books published with information about endangered raptors, probably because Africa's species are dying out at such a phenomenal rate. Nicely illustrated as well.

Terry Tempest Williams, *Refuge*. New York: Random House, 1991. Part memoir, part natural history, this book describes this naturalist's encounters with many threatened or endangered birds of prey near her home state of Utah.

Articles

Tina Adler, "Bringing Back the Birds," *Science News*, August 17, 1996.

Phyllis Berman and Peter Spiegel, "Viva St. Spotted Owl!," *Forbes,* February 12, 1996.

Patrick Bond, "Lesotho Dammed," *Multinational Monitor,* January/February 1997.

Kenneth Brower, "The Naked Vulture and the Thinking Ape," *Atlantic Monthly,* October 1983.

Tui De Roy, "My Treetop Brush with a Harpy," *International Wildlife,* July/August 1998.

Roger Di Silvestro, "What's Killing the Swainson's Hawk," *International Wildlife,* May/June 1996.

Rob Edwards, "Bad Sport: Hundreds of Endangered Birds Are Being Killed to Protect a Countryside Pursuit," *New Scientist,* August 9, 1997.

Shawn Farry, "California Condors Released at Vermilion Cliffs," February 26, 1998. http://www.peregrinefund.org/vermil.html.

Karen Freeman, "Rare Bay Owl Found by Chance," *New York Times,* October 22, 1996.

Daniel Glick, "Disturbing the Peace," *Wilderness,* 1998.

Daniel Glick, "Saving Owls and Jobs Too," *National Wildlife,* August/September 1995.

Laurie Goodrich, "The Place Where Hawk Watching Was Born," *Natural History,* October 1996.

Frank Graham Jr., "100 Years of Conservation," *Audubon,* November/December 1998.

Ernesto Ruelas Inzunza, "Work That Counts," *Natural History,* October 1996.

Verne Kopytoff, "Majestic Species' Fate May Ride on Wings of 6 Freed Condors," *New York Times,* December 10, 1996.

Catherine Lazaroff, "Real Estate Wisdom," *Audubon,* July/ August 1998.

Catherine Lazaroff, "Trouble in the Air," *Audubon,* May/ June 1998.

Richard E. Lewis, "A Rainforest Raptor in Danger," *Oryx,* July 1986.

Les Line, "Giants of the Eagle Kind," *International Wildlife,* July/August 1996.

Les Line, "Lethal Migration," *Audubon,* September/October 1996.

Les Line, "Symbol of Hope?," *National Wildlife,* October/November 1996.

Jessica Maxwell, "River of Raptors," *Natural History,* October 1996.

Robert Mesta, "Condors Return to Arizona," *Endangered Species Bulletin,* November/December 1996.

Dennis J. Money, "The Rochester Peregrine Falcon Project: Private Partnership Brings Birds to Rochester," *New York State Conservationist,* August 1997.

National Parks, "Falcon Returns to the Smokies," January/ February 1998.

Peter Nye, "Where Eagles Soar . . . in New York State," *New York State Conservationist,* December 1996.

Daniel R. Petit, "Partners in Flight: Conserving a Shared Resource," *Endangered Species Technical Bulletin,* March 1995.

Roger Pasquier and Carl Jones, "The Lost and Lonely Birds of Mauritius," *Natural History,* March 1982.

Karen Puracan, "The Philippine Eagle: 'King of Birds,'" *Wildlife Rehabilitation Today,* Spring 1996.

Patrick T. Redig and Harrison B. Tordoff, "Excerpts from the Midwest Peregrine Falcon Restoration, 1994 Report: Plans for 1995 and Beyond," *Raptor Center,* February 26, 1998. www.raptor.cvm.umn.edu/raptor/mpfr1994/ plans.html.

Neil Rettig, "Lords of an Imperiled Realm," *National Geographic,* February 1995.

Galen Rowell, "Peregrines in Peril," *Earth Island Journal,* Spring 1997.

David Seideman, "Whither the Spotted Owl," *Audubon,* March/April 1997.

Noel Snyder, "Captive Breeding of Endangered Species," *Conservation Biology,* April 1996.

Jeff Wheelright, "Condors: Back from the Brink," *Smithsonian,* May 1997.

John Wilkinson, "Good News for Owls and Jobs," *Endangered Species*

Bulletin, November/December 1995.

Martin Williams, "Wings Over East Asia," *Natural History,* October 1996.

Ted Williams, "Back from the Brink: Peregrine Falcon," *Audubon,* November/December 1998.

Ted Williams, "The New Guardians," *Audubon,* January/February 1999.

Ted Williams, "Silent Scourge," *Audubon,* January/February 1997.

Reuven Yosef, "An Oasis in Elat," *Natural History,* October 1996.

Internet Sources

Peregrine Fund, "California Condors Released at Vermillion Cliffs," February 26, 1998. www.peregrinefund.org/ vermil.html.

Peregrine Fund, "Peregrine Fund Returns Panama's National Bird," February 26, 1998. www.peregrinefund.org/harpypr. html.

Peregrine Fund, "Philippine Eagle Conservation," February 26, 1998. www.peregrinefund.org/philipp.html.

The Raptor Center, "Excerpts from the Midwest Peregrine Falcon Restoration," February 26, 1998. www.raptor.cvm.umn. edu/raptor/mpfr1994/plans.html.

Index

Picture Credits

About the Author

Kelly Barth is a freelance writer who lives in Lawrence, Kansas, near the tallgrass prairie, another of the world's "endangered species." In addition to writing, she volunteers at a wildlife rehabilitation clinic where she works with birds of prey.